JAN -

D0367394

SETTING THE RECORD STRAIGHT
THE BOOK
OF MORMON

Cover: The gold plates and the Book of Mormon depict the coming forth of the Book of Mormon from its origin to its completion in fulfillment of Revelation 14:6-7 that the everlasting gospel will go to "every nation, and kindred, and tongue, and people."

SETTING THE RECORD STRAIGHT

THE BOOK
OF MORMON

Jack R. Christianson, Ph.D.

Millennial Press, Inc.
P.O. Box 1741
Orem, UT 84059

ISBN: 1-932597-39-5

Copyright © 2007 Millennial Press

All rights reserved. Reproduction in whole or any parts thereof in any form or by any media without written permission is prohibited. The only exception to this would be the use of brief passages for critical review and analysis. This work is not an official publication of The Church of Latter-day Saints. The views expressed herein are the responsibility of the author and do not necessarily represent the position of the Church or of Millennial Press, Inc.

Cover design and typesetting by Adam Riggs

Dedication

To all who will accept Moroni's promise, found in Moroni 10:4–5, to prayerfully study the Book of Mormon with a sincere heart, with real intent, having faith in Jesus Christ.

Contents

Acknowledgments

It is impossible to thank all those who have influenced the writing of this book. As with all writing projects, it has been a collaborative effort. A special thanks to Randy Bott for his encouragement and friendship. Ryan Bott and Lindsey Shumway at Millennial Press have been more than helpful.

I thank my many students throughout the years who have inspired me and sent me to the scriptures, to the teachings of the living prophets and apostles, to my knees, and to numerous books in order to answer their thoughtful questions concerning the Book of Mormon.

I wish to thank Dennis Largey and Daniel Ludlow for their wonderful "companion" books to the Book of Mormon, as well as numerous other authors. They have enlightened my understanding. I thank the faculty and secretaries at the Orem Institute of Religion. They are a complete inspiration.

I am grateful to my four daughters, their loving husbands, and their children for their constant encouragement, patience, and support. I thank my parents, who regularly asked if I was getting my writing done.

Most of all, I thank my wife, Melanie, for her undying love and support. She has spent much time alone as I have worked on this manuscript. I could never have accomplished the task without her help.

Introduction

As a young man growing up in the heart of Mormon country, I had never thought that people were antagonistic toward the Book of Mormon or Joseph Smith. Nearly everyone with whom I was acquainted was a member of The Church of Jesus Christ of Latter-day Saints. There were, of course, some people in our small Utah community, including some of my family, who had belonged to the Church but chose not to be active or had become disaffected. However, other than a few who whined and complained about the Church controlling everything that happened in the valley, I had never heard hateful or derogatory comments about the Book of Mormon or Joseph Smith.

That all changed when, in the early seventies, I was called to serve a full-time mission for the Church and left the protection of the Wasatch Mountains. I was assigned to a small central-New Mexico town that boasted several denominations that were antagonistic toward the Church, and especially toward Joseph Smith and the Book of Mormon. To find someone who would listen to our message, my companion and I accepted the proposition to attend a special meeting held by one of these churches. We agreed with the woman who invited us that we would come to her services on the condition that she would attend our services as well. She agreed. In our naiveté we did not realize what a mistake we were making. Neither did we realize what a lifelong impact that one decision would have on our lives. I have never been the same since.

The woman graciously attended our service and then she asked if we were intending on keeping our commitment to attend hers. We informed her that we were. She remarked that she was pleased and that her entire congregation was eagerly anticipating our arrival. That should have been a clue, but for two inexperienced nineteen-year-old boys, it was an exciting adventure.

As we entered the meeting hall, the congregation was waiting, along with two empty chairs located at the front. Of course, they were for my companion and me. Much transpired, and the meeting turned ugly for us two Mormon missionaries. We were surrounded and literally mobbed by the congregation. They began to say vile and filthy things concerning Joseph Smith. They screamed that he was a fraud and a liar and that the Book of Mormon was from hell. Their leader announced that the two of us were filled with evil spirits and that everyone should place their hands upon our heads and cast the devils out of us. They were pulling at our clothes and screaming in our ears words that desecrated everything I had ever held sacred concerning the Book of Mormon and Joseph Smith.

Some were so enraged as they attacked Joseph Smith and the Book of Mormon that white foam gathered in the corners of their mouths and spewed from their lips when they spoke. I was terrified and bewildered. Never in my life had I ever considered such things, let alone heard them. It was apparent that they were determined to keep us from leaving until they were through with us. It was very much a nightmare.

At length we escaped and ran to our car. When we did, many followed us and continued their barrage of insults, yelling that unless we left our belief in the Book of Mormon and accepted the "true Jesus," there was no hope for us. They said we would be lost forever if we continued to believe the lie of the Book of Mormon.

We finally made it to our little apartment. Once inside we locked the doors and windows and pulled the blinds. We were shaking. We were scared. We were both somewhat in shock. We knelt and prayed aloud. There was little relief from the dark, foreboding spirit that engulfed each of us and the room like a shroud. We continued to pray, but the darkness remained. There was no relief. Eventually, we split up to pray individually. I prayed in the little living room leaning against a small sofa, and my companion retired to our bedroom.

It was the most difficult night I had ever spent in my young life. Everything I had been taught in my youth about my religious beliefs had not only been challenged but also degraded and dragged through a verbal mire. I knew what I believed was true, but now an entire group of people had assaulted it. I prayed. I cried. I prayed some more. Nothing! I continued through my tears, fears, and depression to ask if what I was doing was true. Was I wasting my time as a missionary? Was I wasting my parents' money? Had I given up my athletic scholarship for a farce? Question after question blasted through my mind. There was no relief.

Again, the thought that I knew the restored gospel was true kept coming into my mind. I would cry out, "I know that I know, but could I know again?" Nothing came. In time, I determined that if I didn't really know that Joseph Smith was a true prophet and that the Book of Mormon was the word of God, then I must return home. I could not teach a lie.

I cannot share what happened during those next few minutes because of its sacred nature. But I assure you that I came to know for myself that night, independent of any other human being on earth, in a grungy little apartment in a little New Mexico town, that the Book of Mormon was true and that

Joseph Smith was a true prophet. From that night until now, I have never been afraid to address any questions or issues surrounding the Book of Mormon. Thus, it is my intent with this small book to set the record straight concerning many, but not all, of the questions and challenges that have continually been brought up regarding the divine origin and teachings of the Book of Mormon.

Since my days as a missionary long ago, I have studied at length the charges leveled against this "book of books" (Pratt, *Autobiography of Parley P. Pratt*, 31), and I have not only discovered them unfounded spiritually but academically as well. I have studied at some of the world's finest universities and have encountered charge after charge against the Book of Mormon while doing so. Not one stands firm. But beyond the intellectual and academic studies, I have experienced for myself—as did Alma, a writer and prophet in the Book of Mormon. He stated in Alma 5:45–46:

"And this is not all. Do ye not suppose that I know of these things myself? Behold, I testify unto you that I do know that these things whereof I have spoken are true. And how do ye suppose that I know of their surety?

"Behold, I say unto you they are made known unto me by the Holy Spirit of God. Behold, I have fasted and prayed many days that I might know these things of myself. And now I do know of myself that they are true; for the Lord God hath made them manifest unto me by his Holy Spirit; and this is the spirit of revelation which is in me."

This is the testimony that is in me. I write this book as a true believer in order to attempt to set the record straight. The material found within its pages comes from accurate and original sources. The views presented come from those who know and live the tenants of The Church of Jesus Christ of Latter-day Saints, not from dissidents or enemies of the Church.

The need to set the record straight appears evident when we view or read what is being produced by those who claim to present a "fair" representation of "Mormon issues," particularly issues surrounding the Book of Mormon. Some of these writers claim that they are simply trying to present all sides of Mormon history, while others claim that they love the Mormons and desire only to save them from being lost or damned by giving allegiance to such a cause as Joseph Smith and the Book of Mormon. This book will address these and other such claims.

I invite each reader to read with a sincere heart and with real intent. As you read, consider the words of Elder Bruce R. McConkie, a former member of the Quorum of the Twelve Apostles of The Church of Jesus Christ of Latter-day Saints. He stated, "There is no greater issue ever to confront mankind in modern times than this: Is the Book of Mormon the mind and will and voice of God?" (*Millennial Messiah*, 179).

A Brief Overview of the Book of Mormon

Before proceeding to the "Frequent Charges and Answers" section of this book, it is necessary, especially for those who have not read the Book of Mormon in its entirety, to offer a brief overview of the book—both historically and doctrinally. This will provide the reader with a better familiarity and a better understanding of terms and explanations provided in the remainder of this text.

The first page of the Book of Mormon, following the "Abbreviations and Designations in Footnotes and Index" page, is the official title of the book. It reads, *The Book of Mormon: Another Testament of Jesus Christ.* And so it is. Its major purpose is contained in its title. The Book of Mormon is another testament of the Savior, Jesus Christ. It is not a history or a story of the Mormons. It is not a replacement for the Bible; it is a companion to the Bible. It is the record of two fallen civilizations that ultimately, chose not to follow Christ and his teachings and thus experienced annihilation.

Of its 6,607 verses, 3,925 make reference to Christ, employing more than one hundred different titles of his name. The writers of the Book of Mormon, then, make reference to some form of Christ's name every 1.7 verses (see Black, *Finding Christ through the Book of Mormon*, 15–16). It is as its introduction states: "The Book of Mormon is a volume of holy scripture comparable to the Bible. It is a record of God's dealings with the ancient inhabitants of the Americas and contains, as does the Bible, the fulness of the everlasting gospel."

The Book of Mormon was written by many ancient prophets. Their words, written on gold plates, were quoted and abridged by a prophet-historian named Mormon. The record gives an account of two great civilizations. One came from Jerusalem in 600 B.C. and afterward separated into two nations, known as the Nephites and the Lamanites. The other came much earlier when the Lord confounded the tongues at the Tower of Babel. This group is known as the Jaredites. After thousands of years, all were destroyed except the Lamanites, and they are the principal ancestors of the American Indians.

The Book of Mormon must not be studied in the same manner as we would study a textbook or a historical novel. It was written, according to its title page, "by the spirit of prophecy and revelation." Therefore, it must be studied in the same manner—prayerfully and spiritually, not simply read like any other book. It is not like other books. It was written with specific purposes in mind. Mainly, those purposes are "to show unto the remnant of the House of Israel what great things the Lord hath done for their fathers; and that they may know the covenants of the Lord, that they are not cast off forever—And also to the convincing of the Jew and Gentile that JESUS is the CHRIST, the ETERNAL GOD, manifesting himself unto all nations" (see title page).

The Book of Mormon came into being as a result of the prayers of the boy Joseph Smith Jr. In 1820 he desired to know which of all the many churches was true. He decided to ask of God and find out for himself after reading James 1:5, which reads, "If any of you lack wisdom, let him ask of God, that giveth to all men liberally, and upbraideth not; and it shall be given him."

He did ask of God, and he received a vision of God the

Father and the resurrected Jesus Christ, the Son. He was told to join none of the existing churches and that he would be an instrument in the hands of God to bring the complete truth to the earth as it had been available anciently (see Joseph Smith–History, 1:7–20).

Three years passed before any further heavenly communication was given. Then, on September 21, 1823, he was visited by an angel from the presence of God who identified himself as Moroni, "the last of the Nephite prophet-historians." Moroni, now a resurrected being, told Joseph of an ancient record engraved on gold plates, deposited in a hill not far from his home. After four years, Joseph was allowed to take the plates and the Urim and Thummim, an instrument of ancient origin, to translate the record (for Biblical accounts of the Urim and Thumim, see Exodus 28:30; Leviticus 8:8; Numbers 27:21; 1 Samuel 28:6). The final product of this translation was titled the Book of Mormon (see Joseph Smith–History, 1:27 65).

The plates were shown to others, including the Three Witnesses and the Eight Witnesses, whose testimonies are found in the preface to the Book of Mormon. The Book of Mormon is divided into fifteen separate books and taken from four different sets of plates—the Plates of Nephi, the Plates of Mormon, the Plates of Ether, and the Brass Plates (see "A Brief Explanation about the Book of Mormon" in its preface pages).

Below is a brief timeline giving the basic chronology of the coming forth of the Book of Mormon.

September 21, 1823

Moroni first appears to Joseph Smith.

1824–1827

Joseph Smith makes four annual visits to the Hill Cumorah to be instructed by Moroni.

October 1825

Joseph works for Josiah Stowell and meets and falls in love with Emma Hale.

January 18, 1827

Joseph Smith and Emma Hale are married.

September 22, 1827

Joseph is entrusted with the gold plates.

February 1828

Martin Harris travels to New York City to show the sacred characters from the plates to Professor Charles Anthon.

February–June 1828

The first 116 pages of the Book of Mormon, known as the Book of Lehi, are translated. Martin Harris then loses the manuscript. It becomes known as the "lost manuscript" (see Doctrine & Covenants 3, 10).

April 7, 1828

Joseph resumes the translation with the help of Oliver Cowdery as his scribe.

September 1828

Joseph regains the gift to translate after losing it for a season.

Fall 1828

Joseph Smith again receives the plates and the Urim and Thummim from Moroni, who took them for a little season.

June 1, 1829

Joseph Smith and Oliver Cowdery move to Fayette, New York, in order to complete the translation of the plates.

Fall–Winter 1829

The Book of Mormon is printed in Palmyra, New York, at the E. B. Grandin Press.

March 26, 1829

The Book of Mormon goes on sale in Palmyra, New York.

The Book of Mormon begins with the story of a prophet named Lehi and his family. The year is approximately 600 B.C. The location is Jerusalem during the reign of King Zedekiah. The family escapes Jerusalem before it is destroyed by the Babylonian empire. They leave without the Brass Plates, which contain a record of the Jews, from the creation of the earth to the writings of the prophet Jeremiah. The plates contained the scriptures of the time and are comparable to the Old Testament today—Genesis to Jeremiah.

Lehi's sons return to Jerusalem to obtain the plates and then the family journeys in the wilderness along the border of the Red Sea. Eventually they build barges to cross the "great waters" (1 Nephi 17:17), arriving somewhere in what is known today as South or Central America. They experience the common vicissitudes of life, including death, family strife, loss of fortune, loss of home, and loss of country. They also experience visions, dreams, and doctrinal teachings by their leaders.

In this first part of the record contained on the Small Plates of Nephi, a major doctrine is taught that assists the reader in understanding the position of The Church of Jesus Christ of Latter-day Saints. The Book of Mormon prophet Nephi declared:

"And we talk of Christ, we rejoice in Christ, we preach of Christ, we prophesy of Christ, and we write according to our prophecies, that our children may know to what source they may look for a remission of their sins" (2 Nephi 25:26).

The Book of Mormon is another testament of Jesus Christ. It teaches of prayer, of the power of scriptures, of the necessity of following prophets of the Lord, of teaching one another the doctrines of Christ, and of how to avoid deception and false teachings. It teaches the importance of enduring to the end and of not giving up on ourselves or on others. The Small Plates of Nephi focus particularly on spiritual teachings, while the Large Plates of Nephi give more of a historical account of the people.

The people divide into two major groups, known as the Nephites and the Lamanites. The Lamanites are marked with a dark skin in order to distinguish them from the Nephites. The two peoples war against each other until the Nephites are destroyed. In the Book of Omni, many years before the extinction of the Nephite nation, the Nephites find another group of people known as the Mulekites, who also had escaped from Jerusalem at the time of King Zedekiah. They followed a man named Mulek, who was one of the sons of Zedekiah (see 2 Kings 19 and 25). The Nephites and the Mulekites become one people.

Mormon, the principal author of the Book of Mormon, writes a short book titled "Words of Mormon," which is placed as a bridge between the Large Plates of Nephi and the Small Plates. The book of Mosiah follows the Words of Mormon and begins the Large Plates, which are filled with teachings of Christ and a story line that engages the reader. It is assumed that the Book of Lehi, which was translated and became the manuscript lost by Martin Harris, was part of the Large Plates and may have been in chronological order just before Mosiah (see Smith, *History of the Church,* 1:21–23; see also Doctrine & Covenants 3, 10).

The books of Alma and Helaman deal mainly with war but are also filled with many doctrinal teachings. They contain stories of conversion as well as the downfall of a nation. Many have questioned why there is so much in the book concerning war. They ask why, if the book is to bring people to Christ, do the writers focus so much on the destruction of war. Gordon B. Hinckley, fifteenth president of The Church of Jesus Christ of Latter-day Saints, gives an insightful reply. He said:

"The war goes on. It is waged across the world over the issues of agency and compulsion. It is waged by an army of missionaries over the issues of truth and error. It is waged in our own lives, day in and day out, in our homes, in our work, in our school associations; it is waged over questions of love and respect, of loyalty and fidelity, of obedience and integrity. We are all involved in it—child, youth, or adult, each of us. We are winning, and the future never looked brighter" ("An Unending Conflict, a Victory Assured," 9).

We are all at war with the evil one on a daily basis. The Book of Mormon's emphasis on war not only helps people of all nations learn how to overcome the devastations of actual, temporal war but also to fight the spiritual war that is going on within the souls of most of us.

The war chapters lead up to the crowning event of the entire book—the coming of the resurrected Lord Jesus Christ to the Book of Mormon people. This coming of Christ and the teachings that he administered to these people led them to nearly two hundred years of peace and prosperity. He chose twelve apostles among them, as he had done in Palestine. He gave the people a discourse similar to the "Sermon on the Mount" speech given in the Old World. He healed their sick and blessed them. Unfortunately, after almost two centuries of peace and a chronic cycle of prosperity and bondage, the Nephites and

Lamanites are divided again and return to war.

The book of Ether, although chronologically the first historical record (about 2,000 B.C.), is placed in the book just before it ends. It was abridged by Moroni and tells of the coming to the Americas of a people who left from the Tower of Babel in the Old Testament. They also experienced destruction because they rejected the prophets of the Lord. The story contained in Ether is a second witness to everything that occurs in the rest of the Book of Mormon. It is a witness of Christ, a witness of the need to follow prophets, a witness of the destructive nature of secret societies and combinations, and a witness of the downfall of a nation that rejects God.

The book ends with the prophet-historian Moroni as the last survivor of the Nephite nation. He gives his last words and some of the teachings of his father, Mormon, and then ends the book with a promise to all seekers of truth:

"Behold, I would exhort you that when ye shall read these things, if it be wisdom in God that ye should read them, that ye would remember how merciful the Lord hath been unto the children of men, from the creation of Adam even down until the time that ye shall receive these things, and ponder it in your hearts.

"And when ye shall receive these things, I would exhort you that ye would ask God, the Eternal Father, in the name of Christ, if these things are not true; and if ye shall ask with a sincere heart, with real intent, having faith in Christ, he will manifest the truth of it unto you, by the power of the Holy Ghost" (Moroni 10:3–5).

Moroni then invites the reader to "come unto Christ, and be perfected in him, and deny yourselves of all ungodliness; and if ye shall deny yourselves of all ungodliness, and love God with all your might, mind and strength, then is his grace sufficient for you, that by his grace ye may be perfect in Christ; and if by the grace of God ye are perfect in Christ, ye can in nowise deny the power of God" (Moroni 10:32).

From its first page to its last page, the focus of the book is to invite all to come unto Christ. Its second major theme is to invite the lost tribes of the House of Israel to come home to the God from which they were scattered.

Frequent Charges and Answers

There certainly are people who know the Book of Mormon more thoroughly than I know it. However, it would be difficult to find anyone who loves the Book of Mormon more than I do. Studying and incorporating its teachings into my life has changed me in nearly every way. I have found what President Hinckley has said on three different occasions to be true. He declared:

"Those who have read [the Book of Mormon] prayerfully, be they rich or poor, learned or unlearned, have grown under its power. . . . Without reservation I promise you that if you will prayerfully read the Book of Mormon, regardless of how many times you previously have read it, there will come into your hearts [and lives and homes] an added measure of the Spirit of the Lord. There will come a strengthened resolution to walk in obedience to his commandments, and there will come a stronger testimony of the living reality of the son of God" ("Power of the Book of Mormon," 6; "An Angel from on High," 9; Ensign, August 2005, 6).

Joseph Smith taught that the Book of Mormon is "the keystone of our religion" (introduction to the Book of Mormon). He also said, "Take away the book of Mormon and the revelations, and where is our religion? We have none" (*History of the Church,* 2:52). Perhaps this is one reason the enemies of the Church of Jesus Christ of Latter-day Saints have worked tirelessly to discredit the Book of Mormon. Disprove the book, and Mormonism is proved to be a fraud. There can be no middle ground when it comes to the Book of Mormon. As Elder Bruce R. McConkie observed, "Either the Book of Mormon is true, or it is false; either it came from God, or it was spawned in the infernal realms. . . . It is not and cannot be simply another treatise on religion; it either came from heaven or from hell" ("What Think Ye of the Book of Mormon?" 73).

Recently I viewed three separate video presentations addressing the LDS faith as well as a marquee sign for a mainstream Christian church, that I have to believe was an internet fabrication. The first film was an anti-LDS DVD production, placed by its producers on the doorsteps of thousands of American homes. The second was a short DVD appealing to disgruntled Latter-day Saints to leave Mormonism and come join with that particular denomination. The third was the PBS special *The Mormons*. The marquee read, "Don't pray about the Book of Mormon, that's how they get you." I was astounded that such an effort had been made to degrade a particular religion's belief system and history in a country founded on principles of religious freedom.

Each of the three video productions focused on the viewpoint and opinions of dissidents from, and enemies of, the Latter-day Saints. If this type of attack had been made upon the Jewish faith or upon Islam or upon a specific race of people, what would the outcry have been? As I watched I could not help but think that if PBS were airing a program on Judaism, it certainly would not interview Muslims to explain their doctrine. Yet that is precisely what occurred in *The Mormons*. Enemies and dissidents gave distorted and unfounded expositions on what Latter-day Saints believe and practice. If the intent of the program were to focus on Islam, would they allow Jews to tell the story and explain the doctrines? The irony of the productions was that they did not focus on anything of which other anti-Mormon projects of the past had not already focused upon.

The message of the marquee, which again, may have been a fabrication, was troubling because it was encouraging each passerby not to pray about the Book of Mormon. Yet the Bible clearly teaches, "If any of you lack wisdom, let him ask of God, that giveth to all men liberally, and abraideth not; and it shall be given him" (James 1:5). Another irony arises with this verse in the Bible. It is the very verse that Joseph Smith read that motivated him to ask God about the various religions of his time. In turn, that prayer led to the coming forth of the Book of Mormon.

I only mention these items because the questions and charges against the Book of Mormon today differ little from those of the 1830s, when the book was published. Time, it appears, does not change the charges. If an individual desires to learn what Latter-day Saints believe, does it not make sense to ask practicing Latter-day Saints who understand and live the tenants of their faith? Does it not make sense to read and pray about the Book of Mormon rather than ask someone or some group with an ax to grind? By going to other sources and individuals, it is as Elder John A. Widtsoe said years ago:

"It is a paradox that men will gladly devote time every day for many years to learn a science or an art, yet will expect to win a knowledge of the gospel, which comprehends all sciences and arts, through perfunctory glances at books or occasional listening to sermons. The gospel should be studied more intensively than any school or college subject. They who pass opinion on the gospel without having given it intimate and careful study are not lovers of truth, and their opinions are worthless"

(*Evidences and Reconciliations*, 1943, 16–17). Thus, there is great need to set the record straight concerning charges leveled against the Book of Mormon.

Peter, one of the original Apostles of Jesus, understood that in the latter times there would be those who would attack and make charges against the truth established by the Lord himself. He taught:

"But there were false prophets also among the people, even as there shall be false teachers among you, who privily shall bring in damnable heresies, even denying the Lord that bought them, and bring upon themselves swift destruction. And many shall follow their pernicious ways; by reason of whom the way of truth shall be evil spoken of" (2 Peter 2:1–2).

We should not be surprised, then, when the same thing happens today by those who feel it is their duty to attack or deride any particular religious belief. If the Book of Mormon is not true, why spend time and energy to fight against those who believe that it is true? Why spend time trying to "interrupt their rejoicings" (Alma 30:22)? Why not let those who believe and have faith in the Book of Mormon do so without incurring the wrath of so many dissidents and enemies? Who cares? If there is no truth in it, then it is as Gamaliel, a doctor of the law in New Testament times, taught concerning the persecution of Peter and John after the death of Jesus. Acts 5:34–42 says of the event:

"Then stood there up one in the council, a Pharisee, named Gamaliel, a doctor of the law, had in reputation among all the people, and commanded to put the apostles forth a little space;

"And said unto them, Ye men of Israel, take heed to yourselves what ye intend to do as touching these men. For before these days rose up Theudas, boasting himself to be somebody; to whom a number of men, about four hundred, joined themselves: who was slain; and all, as many as obeyed him, were scattered, and brought to nought.

"After this man rose up Judas of Galilee in the days of the taxing, and drew away much people after him: he also perished; and all, even as many as obeyed him, were dispersed.

"And now I say unto you, Refrain from these men, and let them alone: for if this counsel or this work be of men, it will come to nought: But if it be of God, ye cannot overthrow it; lest haply ye be found even to fight against God.

"And to him they agreed: and when they had called the apostles, and beaten *them,* they commanded that they should not speak in the name of Jesus, and let them go. And they departed from the presence of the council, rejoicing that they were counted worthy to suffer shame for his name.

"And daily in the temple, and in every house, they ceased not to teach and preach Jesus Christ."

If the Book of Mormon is not true, who cares? It will come to not. Let it alone, as Gamaliel said of Peter and John. But if it is true and it is of God, you cannot overthrow it, "lest haply ye be found even to fight against God." Therefore, as we discuss the various and timeworn charges against the Book of Mormon, it would be wise to refer to Gamaliel's teachings often.

As I attempt to answer many of the objections leveled against the Book of Mormon, please understand that I do not feel obligated to answer every objection. President Ezra Taft Benson clearly taught the position of the Church in such matters: "Our main task is to declare the gospel and do it effectively. We are not obligated to answer every objection. Every man eventually is backed up to the wall of faith, and there he must make his stand" ("A Witness and a Warning," 5).

I provide answers to set the record straight, not to fulfill an obligation to the world or out of fear that by not doing so, people will continue to object or become disaffected from the Church.

President Benson continued: "The only problem the objector has to resolve for himself is whether the Book of Mormon is true. For if the Book of Mormon is true, then Jesus is the Christ, Joseph Smith was his prophet, The Church of Jesus Christ of Latter-day Saints is true, and it is being led today by a prophet receiving revelation" (*A Witness and a Warning*, 4).

To many, this statement may appear oversimplified. Yet ponder for a moment. Is this not precisely what Gamaliel was saying to the persecutors of Peter and John? If the book is true, make the effort to find out and live by its precepts. If it is not true, then it will fade away into obscurity and will not stand the test of time.

Attacks and criticism against the Book of Mormon are not new. Before Joseph Smith had even seen the gold plates from which the Book of Mormon would be translated, he was warned of the intense opposition that would rise against him and the Book of Mormon. On the night of September 21, 1823, Joseph wrote that the Angel Moroni told him that his name would be "had for good and evil among all nations, kindreds, and tongues, or that it should be both good and evil spoken of among all people" (Joseph Smith–History, 1:33).

LDS historian Dean Jessee wrote: "Even though Joseph Smith was warned by a heavenly messenger at an early age that his name would be known for both good and evil among all nations, he was not quite prepared for the intensity of the scorn that was heaped upon him. It was a source of 'serious reflection' to him that one so obscure as he was, whose circumstances made him of 'no consequence in the world,' should attract such bitter opposition ("Among Historians," *Ensign*, September 1979, 57; see also Smith, *History of the Church*, 1:7, 11).

Joseph Smith wrote that once he obtained the plates so

that he could begin translating them, opposition intensified. He wrote:

"For no sooner was it known that I had them, than the most strenuous exertions were used to get them from me. Every stratagem that could be invented was resorted to for that purpose. The persecution became more bitter and severe than before, and multitudes were on the alert continually to get them from me if possible. . . .

"The excitement, however, still continued, and rumor with her thousand tongues was all the time employed in circulating falsehoods about my father's family and myself. If I were to relate a thousandth part of them, it would fill up volumes" (Joseph Smith–History, 1:60–61).

The rumors and falsehoods that existed then are very much with us today. Nearly all of the charges against Joseph Smith today have their origins in much that was written in the mid-1800s and the early 1900s. Because "rumor with her thousand tongues" was so prevalent against the Church, the Book of Mormon, and Joseph himself during the early days, Joseph said, in so many words, that he wanted to set the record straight and leave it up to individuals to determine if he was telling the truth. He wrote:

"Owing to the many reports which have been put in circulation by evil-disposed and designing persons, in relation to the rise and progress of the Church of Jesus Christ of Latter-day Saints, all of which have been designed by the authors thereof to militate against its character as a Church and its progress in the world—I have been induced to write this history, to disabuse the public mind, and put all inquirers after truth in possession of the facts, as they have transpired, in relation both to myself and the Church, so far as I have such facts in my possession.

"In this history I shall present the various events in relation to this Church, in truth and righteousness, as they have transpired, or as they at present exist, being now [1838] the eighth year since the organization of the said Church (Joseph Smith–History 1:1–2).

Published works against the Book of Mormon and the character of Joseph Smith, mainly in relationship to his connection with the Book of Mormon, began even before the Book of Mormon rolled off the E. B. Grandin Press. Dean Jessee provides a detailed list of publications that have been the major sources of today's charges against the Book of Mormon. He wrote:

"But wherever he went, the reaction was the same. In Pennsylvania he was compelled to keep secret the circumstances of the priesthood restoration and his baptism. When the Book of Mormon came off the press, 'great opposition and much persecution followed the believers of its authenticity.' And following the organization of the Church in 1830, 'many false reports, lies, and foolish stories, were published in the newspapers, and circulated in every direction.' So embittered became the public mind 'that the Press [was] universally . . . arrayed against us'" (*History of the Church,* 1:18, 43, 84, 158, 273).

"Among the earliest descriptions of Joseph were those published by Abner Cole, over the name of Obadiah Dogberry, editor of the Palmyra, New York, *Reflector.* Using the E. B. Grandin press, the moonlighting Cole gained unauthorized access to the Book of Mormon manuscript in 1829 and actually published extracts from it in his newspaper until forced to desist by Joseph Smith.

"Miffed at the discovery and forcible discontinuance of his secret enterprise, Cole sought to defame Joseph Smith and his work. He described the Prophet in degrading terms and explained the Book of Mormon as a deception growing out of the family's use of "peep stones" to dig for hidden treasure guarded by evil spirits. He claimed that Joseph concocted the idea of finding a book from the suggestion of a vagabond conjurer named Walters who had participated with the Smiths in their digging ventures."

"Cole laid the groundwork for the theme of deception, indolence, and irreligion that was to characterize descriptions of Joseph Smith in subsequent non-Mormon writings. But while early newspapers labeled Joseph Smith as an unprincipled character, it was Eber D. Howe's book, *Mormonism Unvailed,* in 1834 that canonized that theme for future non-Mormon discussions. Howe's work was the culmination of efforts of a Kirtland, Ohio, anti-Mormon committee spearheaded by an embittered ex-Mormon, Philastus Hurlbut, cut off from the Church for immorality. Having been restrained by court injunction from committing personal violence upon Joseph Smith, Hurlbut undertook to vent his wrath by prospecting for information that would 'divest Joseph Smith of all claims to the character of an honest man, and place him at an immeasurable distance from the high station which he pretends to occupy. The result consisted of affidavits signed by eighty-two New York and Pennsylvania residents who claimed personal knowledge derogatory to the Smith character. The affidavits portrayed Joseph Smith as 'lazy, intemperate, 'entirely destitute of moral character and addicted to vicious habits,' including the deceptive practice of digging for hidden treasure. The legal framework of the documents gave them a strong flavor of credibility in an age uncritical of its information.

"With the exception of I. Woodbridge Riley's work, *The Founder of Mormonism: A Psychological Study of Joseph Smith, Jr.,* (1902) in which the author sought to examine Joseph Smith's character from the standpoint of psychology, almost every significant non-Mormon study of Joseph Smith from 1834 to the present has used the Hurlbut framework. Besides

Howe's book, these include William Harris, *Mormonism Portrayed* (1841); John A. Clark, *Gleanings by the Way* (1842); John C. Bennett, *The History of the Saints, or, An Expose of Joe Smith and Mormonism* (1842); Henry Caswall, *The Prophet of the Nineteenth Century* (1843); William S. Parrott, *The Veil Uplifted* (1865); Pomeroy Tucker, *Origin, Rise, and Progress of Mormonism* (1867); J. H. Kennedy, *Early Days of Mormonism* (1888); Thomas Gregg, *The Prophet of Palmyra* (1890); Lu. B. Cake, *Peepstone Joe and the Peck Manuscript* (1899); Charles A. Shook, *The True Origin of Mormon Polygamy* (1914); William A. Linn, *The Story of the Mormons* (1923); Harry M. Beardsley, *Joseph Smith and His Mormon Empire* (1931); and Fawn M. Brodie, *No Man Knows My History: The Life of Joseph Smith the Mormon Prophet* (1945).

"For these writers, the Hurlbut thesis, to use Thomas Gregg's words, furnished 'irresistible proof' that Joseph Smith's character 'was such as would render it preposterous and impossible that he should have been selected through divine agency to carry a God-given revelation to mankind and lead in a great reformation'" (Jessee, "Among Historians," 57–59).

From the above excerpts, it is evident that the opposition to the Book of Mormon and Joseph Smith is richly based upon the writings of enemies and dissidents. On the other hand, generally, when sources are quoted from LDS Church writings, they are almost always taken out of context and used to support ideas or doctrines that were not intended by the original authors.

In the next several pages we will discuss some of the charges and the answers to those charges from the doctrines and teachings of the Church, as they were intended to be understood. I alone am responsible for this material. I do not officially represent The Church of Jesus Christ of Latter-day Saints with these answers. They are from my research and understanding and in no way have been authorized or condoned by Church authorities.

1. The Spalding Theory.

The Charge: Joseph Smith used the nineteenth century unpublished novel "Manuscript Found," by Solomon Spalding, as his source for writing the Book of Mormon.

The Answer: The Spalding theory is not considered a plausible explanation for the origin of the Book of Mormon by most Book of Mormon critics today, but it was a common anti-Mormon theme for approximately fifty years. It was the invention of the dissident and excommunicated Latter-day Saint Philastis Hurlbut and was first published in 1834 in *Mormonism Unvailed*, by E. D. Howe. This book presented the theory that Joseph Smith plagiarized the Book of Mormon by stealing the ideas for the storyline from Solomon Spalding.

Spalding (1761–1816) was a Revolutionary War veteran, a former Calvinist minister, a graduate of Dartmouth College and the would-be author of the "Manuscript Story," a prehistoric American epic story explaining the lost civilization of the mound builders. This unfinished story bears only occasional resemblance to the Book of Mormon text and is not claimed by many literary critics as having formed the basis for the LDS scripture (see "Spalding Theory", *Book of Mormon Reference Companion*, 734-735).

Dr. Kent P. Jackson has written concerning the unfounded claims of the Solomon Manuscript: "Its popularity waned, however, when the manuscript resurfaced in 1884 in Honolulu, and readers were able to observe that Spalding's novel had nothing in common with the Book of Mormon. It has almost no religious content, the language is utterly unlike that of the Book of Mormon, the storyline bears no resemblance, and no historical connection can be established between Joseph Smith and the manuscript" (Largey, *Book of Mormon Reference Companion*, 735).

This overused and unfounded argument against the Book of Mormon holds little substance. To review this manuscript and see how utterly ridiculous this argument is, look for it online. Then read the Book of Mormon from cover to cover, and you will see that there is nothing that connects the two manuscripts and that Joseph Smith did not use anything written by Solomon Spaulding. Spaulding died when Joseph Smith was eleven years old. There is no evidence that the two ever met or that Joseph was even aware of the existence of the Spaulding Manuscript in his lifetime.

When considering this theory and others of like manner that claim Joseph Smith wrote the Book of Mormon himself or copied work written by others, it should be remembered that he claimed to have translated the book from the gold plates by the gift and power of God. It should also be remembered that he had very little formal education. In fact, when Joseph's wife Emma was asked, many years after his death, if he could have written the story privately, then dictated it, pretending he was translating from the plates, she replied, "Joseph Smith could neither write nor dictate a coherent and well-worded letter; let alone dictating a book like the Book of Mormon . . . it is marvelous to me . . . as much as to anyone. . . . I am satisfied that no man could have dictated the writing of the manuscripts unless he was inspired; for, when [I was] acting as his scribe, [he] would dictate to me for hour after hour; and when returning from meals, or after interruptions, he would at once begin where he had left off, without either seeing the manuscript or having any portion of it read to him." Emma continued, "It would have been improbable that a learned man could do this, and, for one so ignorant and unlearned as he was, it was simply impossible" (Newell and Avery, *Mormon Enigma*, 26). Therefore, it would have been exceptionally difficult, if not impossible, for one so young and uneducated to write such a complex book integrating hundreds of biblical references, numerous story lines, doctrinal exhortations, various writing styles, Near eastern cultural references, etcetera and do it in less than ninety days total writing time. Ludlow, in his *A Companion to Your Study of the Book of Mormon,* quoted Francis Kirkham about the time it took to finish the translation of the book. He wrote, "It appears that the entire copy might have been prepared before the printing began for the reason that the original copy would be kept at a separate place to guard against loss or destruction. In any event, one month to six or seven weeks would be no more than sufficient time to prepare the manuscript, arrange for, and actually begin the printing which, from the evidence presented below, began in August, 1829.

The conclusion is this:

The translation and writing of the Book of Mormon commenced April 7, 1829, at page sixteen or a little before and were completed about July 1, 1829. . . . The evidence appears complete, that the printing of the Book of Mormon began in August, 1829, and was completed not later than March 26, 1830, at the printing press of E. B. Grandin at Palmyra, New York. From the above sources, it is clear that the Book of Mormon was dictated by Joseph Smith in the relatively short period of seventy-five working days. There were many witnesses both at his home at Harmony, Pennsylvania, and at Fayette, New York. Many persons knew all the facts. No one has attempted to deny them. The physical facts concerning time, place and scribes of the writing of the translation and the publishing of the Book of Mormon are attested by both believers and nonbelievers in the divine origin of the book. There was no incentive for deception or misrepresentation of these facts by the persons who willingly gave their time to this effort. No wealth, honor, power or influence was to come to any one of them from this achievement only the privilege to serve. The reward was joy in this life and in eternity by helping to lead "save it be but one soul" into the way of divine love and eternal progress" (Ludlow, *A Companion to Your Study of the Book of Mormon, 32*).

I have had the privilege of writing numerous books in my lifetime. I have obtained advanced degrees. Yet, I could not write a book of over five hundred pages with such complexity and spirit in seventy five working days. Not even close. I know of no human being who could accomplish such a task without divine help. The only way Joseph Smith could have done it was to have done by the gift and power of God just as he said. Therefore, it would be helpful and wise for any seeker of truth to read the book carefully and prayerfully then ask one simple question; could any man, without divine guidance, have written this book?

2. The Use of a Seer Stone in the Bottom of a Hat.

The Charge: Joseph Smith used a mysterious seer stone in the bottom of a hat to not only to translate the Book of Mormon but also to find hidden treasure.

The Answer: Evidence shows that Joseph Smith did have in his possession a seer stone that he found while digging a well in company with his brother Hyrum for a Mr. Clark Chase, near Palmyra, New York. Oliver Cowdery said of his role in the translation of the Book of Mormon: "I wrote with my own pen the entire Book of Mormon (save a few pages), as it fell from the lips of the Prophet Joseph Smith, as he translated by the gift and power of God, by the means of the Urim and Thummim, or, as they are called by that book, 'Holy Interpreters'" (Roberts, *Comprehensive History of the Church,* 1:128–29).

"Neither Joseph Smith nor his principal scribe, Oliver Cowdery, mentioned a 'seer stone' in the translation work, but they repeatedly indicate the use of the Urim and Thummim" (*Book of Mormon Reference Companion*, 712). Joseph Smith declared that he translated the Book of Mormon "through the medium of the Urim and Thummim . . . by the gift and power of God" (*History of the Church*, 4:537).

The Urim and Thummim was described by Joseph as a "curious instrument . . . which consisted of two transparent stones set in the rim of a bow fastened to a breastplate" (*History of the Church*, 4:537; see also Joseph Smith–History 1:59). Joseph's mother, Lucy Mack Smith, described the instrument as "consist[ing] of two smooth three cornered diamonds set in glass, and the glasses were set in silver bows, which were connected with each other in much the same way as old fashioned spectacles" (Smith, *Biographical Sketches*, 101).

In 1887 David Whitmer said that Joseph Smith used a seer stone as well as the Urim and Thummim while translating the Book of Mormon. Objectors to the Book of Mormon take his statement about the hat and use it to make Joseph appear mystical and involved in some occult practice of his day. Yet, when taken in context, Whitmer's statement is not so mystical. In his *Address to all Believers in Christ*, he stated:

"At times when brother Joseph would attempt to translate he would look into the hat in which the stone was placed [to exclude the light], he found he was spiritually blind and could not translate. He told us his mind dwelt too much on earthly things, and various causes would make him incapable of proceeding with the translation. When in this condition he would go out and pray, and when he became sufficiently humble before God, he could then proceed with the translation. Now we see how very strict the Lord is, and how he requires the heart of man to be just right in his sight before he can receive revelation from him" (Roberts, *Comprehensive History of the Church*, 1:130–31).

By his statement about the hat and the seer stone, it is clear that Whitmer was referring to the delicate process of revelation and not focusing on magic or the occult. Yet Book of Mormon detractors beat the seer stone and the mysterious hat discussion to death.

Joseph Fielding McConkie and Craig J. Ostler, in their book *Revelations of the Restoration,* give six reasons why Whitmer's account of the seer stone being used in a hat to translate the Book of Mormon cannot be taken seriously as conclusive evidence of the translation process. I quote extensively from their work because it is precisely what I have discovered in my research. That is, that Joseph Smith used the Urim and Thummim to translate the Book of Mormon rather than the seer stone that was in his possession.

They write that the reported account of David Whitmer, concerning the translation process clearly contradicts the principles established by the Lord in Section Nine of the Doctrine and Covenants. It is also at odds with the testimonies of both Joseph Smith and Oliver Cowdery. McConkie and Ostler conclude that it is not a reliable source on this matter. They are entirely respectful of and grateful for the testimony to which David Whitmer appended his name as one of the Three Witnesses of the truthfulness of the Book of Mormon and its divine origin. That, however, does not make him a competent witness to the process of translation. As to David Whitmer's explanation, it should be remembered that there is no record that he ever looked into the Urim and Thummim, or that he ever translated anything. His testimony of how the Book of Mormon was translated is simply hearsay.

Cook wrote that for a period spanning twenty years (1869–88), some seventy recorded testimonies about the coming forth of the Book of Mormon claim David Whitmer as their source. These accounts were filled with inconsistencies. They repeatedly reported Whitmer to have said that after the loss of the 116 pages, the Lord took both the plates and the Urim and Thummim from the Prophet and never returned them. In their stead, Whitmer maintained, the Prophet used an oval-shaped, chocolate-colored seer stone slightly larger than an egg for the translation process. Thus, everything we have in the Book of Mormon, according to Whitmer, was translated by placing the chocolate-colored stone in a hat into which Joseph would bury his head so as to close out the light. While doing so he could see "an oblong piece of parchment, on which the hieroglyphics would appear," and below the ancient writing, the translation would be given in English. Joseph would then read this to Oliver Cowdery, who in turn would write it. If he did so correctly, the characters and the interpretation would disappear and be replaced by other characters with their interpretation (Cook, *David Whitmer Interviews*, 115, 157–58).

McConkie and Ostler wrote that such an explanation is simply fiction created for the purpose of demeaning Joseph Smith and to undermine the validity of the revelations he received after translating the Book of Mormon. The six reasons they give for this claim are listed below.

"First, for more than fifty years David Whitmer forthrightly rejected Joseph Smith, declaring him to be a fallen prophet. Though he never denied his testimony of the Book of Mormon, he rejected virtually everything else associated with the ministry of Joseph Smith and the restoration of the gospel. His rejection included both the Aaronic and Melchizedek Priesthoods, which were restored during the time the Book of Mormon was being translated and, of course, the revelations which would eventually constitute the Doctrine and Covenants.

"Second, according to David Whitmer's account of how the Book of Mormon was translated, Joseph Smith was the instrument of transmission, while translation rested solely with the Lord. This is simply a reflection of the notion of divine dictation, which holds that every word of scripture comes from God himself. If David Whitmer's account is to be accepted, revelation also includes spelling and punctuation. This notion is at odds with the explanation found in Doctrine and Covenants 8 and 9, which details how revelation comes. In this respect, Richard Anderson observed that Whitmer, 'after decades of reflection outside of the Church, concluded that no modification could possibly be made in any revelation. This highly rigid view of these revelations matched his highly rigid view of the origin of the Book of Mormon' ("By the Gift and Power of God," 84). By contrast Brigham Young observed, 'Should the Lord Almighty send an angel to rewrite the Bible, it would in many places be very different from what it now is. And I will even venture to say that if the Book of Mormon were now to be rewritten, in many instances it would materially differ from the present translation' (*Journal of Discourses,* 9:311).

"David Whitmer repeatedly said that if a word was misspelled, the translator would not be able to go on until it had been corrected. This hardly allows for the 3,913 changes that have been made between the first edition of the Book of Mormon and the edition presently in use.

"Third, if the process of translation was simply a matter of reading from a seer stone in a hat, surely Oliver Cowdery could do that as well, if not better, than Joseph Smith. After all, Oliver was a schoolteacher. How then do we account for Oliver's inability to translate? Further, regarding the use of a hat in translation, Joseph's brother William Smith explained that the Prophet used the Urim and Thummim attached to the breastplate by a rod that held the seer stones set in the rims of a bow before his eyes. 'The instrument caused a strain on Joseph's eyes, and he sometimes resorted to covering his eyes with a hat to exclude the light in part' (Smith, "Rod of Iron" 1, 3 [February 1924]: 7).

"Fourth, Joseph Smith repeatedly testified to having both the plates and the Urim and Thummim returned to him. He further testified that he translated from the plates by the use of the Urim and Thummim.

"Fifth, David Whitmer gave inconsistent accounts of the instrument used to translate. Thomas Wood Smith, in a published response about an interview he had with David Whitmer, who told him that Joseph Smith used the Urim and Thummim in translating the Book of Mormon, wrote, 'When I first read Mr. Traughber's paper in the Herald of November 15th, I thought that I would not notice his attack at all, as I supposed that I was believed by the Church to be fair and truthful in my statements of other men's views, when I have occasion to use them, and I shall make this reply only: That unless my interview with David Whitmer in January, 1876, was only a dream, or that I failed to understand plain English, I believed then, and since, and now, that he said that Joseph possessed, and used the Urim and Thummim in the translation of the inscriptions referred to, and I remember being much pleased with that statement, as I had heard of the 'Seer stone' being used. And unless I dreamed the interview, or very soon after failed to recollect the occasion, he described the form and size of the said Urim and Thummim. The nearest approach to a retraction of my testimony as given . . . publicly in many places from the stand from January, 1876, till now, is, that unless I altogether misunderstood 'Father Whitmer' on this point, he said the translation was done by the aid of the Urim and Thummim. If he says he did not intend to convey such an impression to my mind, then I say I regret that I misunderstood him, and unintentionally have misrepresented him. But that I understood him as represented by me frequently I still affirm" (as cited in Cook, "David Whitmer Interviews," 56).

"Finally, the testimony of David Whitmer simply does not accord with the divine pattern. If Joseph Smith translated everything that is now in the Book of Mormon without using the gold plates, we are left to wonder why the plates were necessary in the first place. It will be remembered that possession of the plates placed the Smith family in considerable danger, causing them a host of difficulties. If the plates were not part of the translation process, this would not have been the case. It also leaves us wondering why the Lord directed the writers of the Book of Mormon to make a duplicate record of the plates of Lehi. This provision—which compensated for the loss of the 116 pages—would have served no purpose either. Further, we would be left to wonder why it was necessary for Moroni to instruct Joseph each year for four years before he was entrusted with the plates. We would also wonder why it was so important for Moroni to show the plates to the Three Witnesses, including David Whitmer. And why did the Lord have the Prophet show the plates to the Eight Witnesses? Why all this flap and fuss if the Prophet didn't really have the plates and if they were not used in the process of translation? What David Whitmer is asking us to believe is that the Lord had Moroni seal up the plates and the means by which they were to be translated hundreds of years before they would come into Joseph Smith's possession and then decided to have the Prophet use a seer stone found while digging a well so that none of these things would be necessary after all. Is this, we would ask, really a credible explanation of the way the heavens operate?" (*Revelations of the Restoration*, 95–98).

Elder Joseph Fielding Smith, who later would become president of the Church, had deep feelings in contrast to what Roberts and Whitmer said concerning the translation process.

He held fast to the account given by Joseph Smith and Oliver Cowdery. He wrote:

"While the statement has been made by some writers that the Prophet Joseph Smith used a *seer stone* part of the time in his translating of the record, and information points to the fact that he did have in his possession such a stone, yet there is no authentic statement in the history of the Church which states that the use of such a stone was made in that translation. The information is all *hearsay*, and personally, I do not believe that the stone was used for that purpose. The reason I give for this conclusion is found in the statement of the Lord to the Brother of Jared as recorded in Ether 3:22–24.

"I feel it is important to include these Book of Mormon verses here in order to keep these statements by Elder Smith in proper context.

"And behold, when ye shall come unto me, ye shall write them and shall seal them up, that no one can interpret them; for ye shall write them in a language that they cannot be read.

"And behold, these two stones will I give unto thee, and ye shall seal them up also with the things which ye shall write.

"For behold, the language which ye shall write I have confounded; wherefore I will cause in my own due time that these stones shall magnify to the eyes of men these things which ye shall write."

President Smith continued, "These stones, the Urim and Thummim, which were given to the Brother of Jared, were preserved for this *very purpose of translating the record*, both of the Jaredites and the Nephites. The Prophet was impressed by Moroni with the fact that these stones were given for that very purpose (see Joseph Smith–History 1:34–45). It hardly seems reasonable to suppose that the Prophet would substitute something evidently *inferior* under these circumstances. It may have been so, but it is so easy for a story of this kind to be circulated because of the fact that the Prophet did possess a seer stone, which he may have used for some other purposes" (Smith, *Doctrines of Salvation*, 3:225–26).

The story then, of the stone in the hat is very likely just that—a story. There is no conclusive evidence that Joseph Smith used that process in the translation of the Book of Mormon. We do, however, have evidence that Joseph Smith did have a seer stone and that he gave the stone to Oliver Cowdery. David Whitmer stated that after the death of Oliver Cowdery in 1848, Phineas Young, brother to Brigham Young, received the seer stone from Oliver's widow while on a visit to Missouri. He in turn, on his arrival back in Salt Lake City, gave the stone to Brigham Young. The stone has remained in the possession of the Church since that time (see *Book of Mormon Reference Companion*, 712).

As to the charge that Joseph Smith used the seer stone to locate hidden treasure, it is almost laughable. Joseph was instructed from the very beginning that "Satan would try to tempt me (in consequence of the indigent circumstances of my father's family), to get the plates for the purpose of getting rich. This he forbade me, saying that I must have no other object in view in getting the plates but to glorify God, and must not be influenced by any other motive than that of building his kingdom; otherwise I could not get them" (Joseph Smith–History 1:46). Joseph's entire objective was to glorify God and build his Kingdom.

If obtaining riches was Joseph's objective in having the seer stone, then he was terribly unsuccessful. He struggled financially most of his life. He was told by the Lord in July of 1830 that "in temporal labors thou shalt not have strength, for this is not thy calling" (D&C 24:9). Another question that must be asked is, if Joseph had used the seer stone to find hidden treasures of silver and gold, why did he not live like some of the other ministers of his day? Why did he not have a home of his own until the Nauvoo period? (The homestead cabin in Nauvoo was Joseph and Emma's first home. They moved into the cabin in May 1839). Why did he or his family not prosper from the sale of the Book of Mormon? There is no evidence that Joseph earned any money from the sale of the Book of Mormon. Yet according to various Web sources listing the "Best Selling Single Volume Books of All Time," the Book of Mormon is listed eighth in the world with over 120,000,000 copies sold to date. Again, Joseph never received any financial gain nor has the Church, from Book of Mormon sales.

If he was in it for the money, why did Joseph have to borrow fifty dollars from Martin Harris in 1829 to travel to Pennsylvania (see Joseph Smith–History 1:61)? Why did Martin Harris mortgage his farm for three thousand dollars in order to secure publication of the first five thousand leather-bound copies of the Book of Mormon in 1829 (see *Book of Mormon Reference Companion*, 134)? The charge that Joseph Smith used the seer stone to gain wealth is preposterous. There is absolutely no evidence to substantiate this charge.

3. No Archeological Evidence

The Charge: There is no archaeological evidence that the Book of Mormon people or geographical locations ever existed.

The Answer: Each time I am confronted with this charge or hear it presented in a film I am astounded. Reasonable, respectable people all across the earth claim that there is no proof that can allow for a belief in the Book of Mormon. They claim that there is no archaeological evidence that can substantiate Joseph Smith's story of the coming forth of the Book of Mormon. Yet many of these same people attest to a belief in a God for whom there is no archaeological evidence to substantiate their belief. (I believe that the earth itself is evidence of His existence).

"All things denote there is a God; yea even the earth, and all things that are on the face of it, yea and its motion, yea and also all the planets which move in their regular form do witness that there is a Supreme Creator" (Alma 30:44). However, none of that is archaeological in nature; rather, it is spiritual. Millions continue to believe in God and worship Him as the center of their lives without archaeological evidence. Why is it so difficult to do the same with the Book of Mormon?

The very existence of the Book of Mormon itself is its own best evidence of its authenticity. The one fact that the scoffer must deal with is that the book exists and millions adhere to its teachings. John E. Clark, a professor of anthropology, suggests, "For open-minded inquirers, the materiality of the book and the remarkable consistency of its narrative are sufficient grounds for taking the book seriously and considering its truthfulness. But the ultimate question of truthfulness is a spiritual one requiring faith in the possibility of a spiritual answer from a divine source" (*Book of Mormon Reference Companion*, 72). Those who are sincere in their inquiry can come to know for themselves if the Book of Mormon is true. As previously quoted in the introduction, they can follow the promise contained at the end of the book, in Moroni 10:3–5, which reads:

"Behold, I would exhort you that when ye shall read these things, if it be wisdom in God that ye should read them, that ye would remember how merciful the Lord hath been unto the children of men, from the creation of Adam even down until the time that ye shall receive these things, and ponder it in your hearts.

"And when ye shall receive these things, I would exhort you that ye would ask God, the Eternal Father, in the name of Christ, if these things are not true; and if ye shall ask with a sincere heart, with real intent, having faith in Christ, he will manifest the truth of it unto you, by the power of the Holy Ghost.

"And by the power of the Holy Ghost ye may know the truth of all things."

Clark declares further, "Believers who put stock in physical evidences confuse the real basis of their belief. Testimony from the earth follows that from the heavens" (*Ibid.*).

Having laid the groundwork for the fact that the only way we can come to know of the truthfulness of the Book of Mormon is from a heavenly source, I can now discuss some of the archaeological evidence that does exist. Archaeology, of course, is the study of material remains left by past civilizations and peoples. Archaeologists have the ominous task of finding convincing, confirmable evidence for that which is described and written about within the text being studied. This is no easy task for the Bible or the Book of Mormon. Numerous problems exist in trying to do so.

In 1830, when the Book of Mormon came off the press, much of today's archaeological findings in North, Central, and South America had not been discovered. Since that time, numerous cities have been unearthed, along with evidence of previous civilizations. Many of the debates over archaeological evidence have risen because specific items of significance have not been discovered, though many have. According to author John Sorenson, there have been massive clues of geographical, historical, and cultural evidence overlooked while seeking the smaller individual evidences. He suggests that the physical geography of southern Mexico and Guatemala, including the relative mountains, hills, rivers, plains, farm land, waste lands, oceans, and so forth have been shown to match reasonably well with the narrative in the Book of Mormon (see *Book of Mormon Reference Companion*, 71).

The Stella 5 stone found in southern Mexico is estimated to be dated between 200 B.C. and 300 B.C. The stone portrays a busy scene of humans and other beings surrounding a large fruit tree. Many LDS scholars believe the tree to be a representation of the tree of life found in 1 Nephi 8 and 11. Others disagree because of no accompanying written explanation of the stone and believe this interpretation should be left open for broader interpretation. Broader interpretation or not, the point is that a large stone has been discovered that depicts scenes from one of the central stories contained in the Book of Mormon.

There are similar items and animals mentioned in the Book of Mormon that cause scholars to debate the existence of the Book of Mormon people occupying the Americas that are described in the book. They include the people having horses, elephants, and silk, iron, steel, and gold plates (see *Book of Mormon Reference Companion*, 71). The question concerning where the gold plates are today will be discussed in the next charge and answer section.

What do those who claim that there is no archeological evidence for the Book of Mormon do with the common story held by numerous modern peoples in the Americas as well as past cultures and civilizations of the visit of a great white God to their forefathers? The legend of Quetzalcoatl, the white, bearded god, who visited the Americas, is had among many people and there are several variations of the story. The name Quetzalcoatl is the name of prominent deity and king of ancient Mexico. It means serpent and feathered. The tradition was had among the Mayan and Aztec peoples and is found mentioned in records as far back as 1000-500 B.C. (see, Allen, *Book of Mormon Reference Companion*, 668).

The crowning event in the Book of Mormon is found in Third Nephi chapters 11-28 when the resurrected Savior, Jesus Christ, descends from heaven and teaches the Book of Mormon people for several days in the Americas in 34 A.D. He blesses and heals their sick, performs miracles and gives a sermon similar to the Sermon on the Mount. He calls twelve apostles and establishes His church in the same manner as He did in the New Testament. It is difficult to explain away the traditions of the people of the Americas and beautiful story contained in the Book of Mormon.

Again, John E. Clark, referring to John Sorenson's work explains:

"Similarly, many of the cultural elements, practices, metaphors, and allusions in the latter part of the Book of Mormon appear to be Mesoamerican. These include such things as writing and record keeping, cannibalism, large-scale warfare, human sacrifice, conquest of cities by capturing the central "tower," or pyramid (Moroni 9:7), combat weaponry, cotton armor (Alma 49:6), metaphors for the countenance of god in statuary (Alma 5), representations of trees growing out of human hearts (Alma 32), a directional system of four quarters, pagan beliefs of gods inhabiting an underworld (Alma 18:31), and many other items (see Sorenson, *Images*). Moreover, the chronology of the rise and fall of civilized peoples, the relative locations of these civilizations, and the extreme fluctuations in populations recorded in the Book of Mormon correspond reasonably well with those reconstructed archaeologically in the past thirty years for Middle America" (*Book of Mormon Reference Companion*, 71).

Again, one of the major problems encountered in seeking archaeological evidence in trying to prove the validity of a scriptural text is using human and earthly standards of judgment to try to prove heavenly and spiritual writings. President Gordon B. Hinckley put the issue into spiritual terms when he said, "The evidence for [the Book of Mormon's] truth, for its validity in a world that is prone to demand evidence, lies not in archaeology or anthropology, though these may be helpful to some. It lies not in word research or historical analysis, though these may be confirmatory. The evidence for its truth and validity lies within the covers of the book itself. The test of its truth lies in reading it" ("The Cornerstones of Our Faith," 52).

4. Where Are the Gold Plates Today?

The Charge: If the Book of Mormon is true, where is the original manuscript (the gold plates) from which the Book of Mormon was translated?

The Answer: Where is the original manuscript for the Holy Bible? To my knowledge there is none. Yet millions of people continue to believe in the Bible as the word of God, including me. In fact, for many Christians today, the Bible is final, infallible, and forever. Some sources, found on the Web, have lists of "Best Selling Books" that set the number of Bibles sold to date as high as between five and six billion copies.

When answering this question about the golden plates, it would be well to ask another question. Where is the Ark of the Covenant that was used by ancient Israel? According to the book of Revelation in the New Testament, it is not hidden in some army warehouse, as portrayed by Steven Spielberg and George Lucas in their film *Raiders of the Lost Ark*. It was taken back into the presence of God. Revelation 11:19 reads: "And the temple of God was opened in heaven, and there was seen in his temple the ark of his testament: and there were lightnings, and voices, and thunderings, and an earthquake, and great hail."

Why, then, is it difficult for people to believe Joseph Smith when he said that the Angel Moroni, who had given him the gold plates, also took them back when the work of translation was completed? Joseph Smith recorded in his history, "When, according to arrangements, the messenger called for them, I delivered them up to him; and he has them in his charge until this day, being the second day of May, one thousand eight hundred and thirty-eight" (Joseph Smith–History 1:60).

Would having the gold plates for investigators to view in a museum make a difference in their acceptance of the Book of Mormon as the word of God? Perhaps it might for some. However, it has been my experience as a teacher and as an educational sociologist, that for the majority, it is likely that seeing the plates would not necessarily enhance their believing of the story of the coming forth of the Book of Mormon. Modern museums and galleries are full of artifacts that give physical evidence to historical events that many do not believe because they have been taught otherwise. I am acquainted with an individual, for example, who does not believe that the Holocaust occurred. This individual claims that it is nothing more than American propaganda. Why? Because this person was taught as a youth that the Americans were trying to brainwash the world into believing that it actually took place. Yet, how can people not believe when they see the evidence and listen to the stories of those who saw it, lived it and lost their families in it?

Is it the same with the golden plates and those who saw them, lifted them and even died themselves or lost family members because of them? Has it ever occurred to the reader that all Joseph and Hyrum Smith had to say was that they did not really see the angel and there really were no gold plates? This would have saved their lives from the hands of their assassins. All Joseph had to say was that he was kidding. That he did not see the Father and the Son. That, he did not see visions and the Book of Mormon was not true; it was all a hoax. Instead, what he did say was, "I had actually seen a light, and in the midst of that light I saw two Personages, and they did in reality speak to me; and though I was hated and persecuted for saying that I had seen a vision, yet it was true; and while they were persecuting me, reviling me, and speaking all manner of evil against me falsely for so saying, I was led to say in my heart: Why persecute me for telling the truth? I have actually seen a vision; and who am I that I can withstand God, or why does the world think to make me deny what I have actually seen? For I had seen a vision; I knew it, and I knew that God knew it, and I could not deny it, neither dared I do it; at least I knew that by so doing I would offend God, and come under condemnation" (Joseph Smith-History 1:25).

If people choose not to believe those who were martyred for their testimonies (Joseph and Hyrum Smith) that is one thing, but why is it difficult to believe others, who had nothing to gain by giving their testimonies to the world that the plates were real? At least eleven men, besides Joseph and Hyrum, saw and handled the plates, but many people scoff at their testimony. In any legal setting, would not the testimony of eleven eyewitnesses be enough to prove the case? Why not with the Book of Mormon? The Apostle Paul taught, "In the mouth of two or three witnesses shall every word be established" (2 Corinthians 13:1). Then why would a believer in the Bible not accept the witness of eleven individuals? It does not make sense.

In the opening pages of the preface to the Book of Mormon, the testimony of the Three Witnesses—Oliver Cowdery, David Whitmer, and Martin Harris—is given in clarity. Their testimony of the gold plates is followed by that of the Eight Witnesses— Christian Whitmer, Jacob Whitmer, Peter Whitmer Jr., John Whitmer, Hiram Page, Joseph Smith Sr., Hyrum Smith, and Samuel Smith. Their testimonies read as follows:

THE TESTIMONY OF THREE WITNESSES

"BE IT KNOWN unto all nations, kindreds, tongues, and people, unto whom this work shall come: That we, through the grace of God the Father, and our Lord Jesus Christ, have seen the plates which contain this record, which is a record of the people of Nephi, and also of the Lamanites, their brethren, and also of the people of Jared, who came from the tower of which hath been spoken. And we also know that they have been translated by the gift and power of God, for his voice hath declared it unto us; wherefore we know of a surety that the work is true. And we also testify that we have seen the engravings which are upon the plates; and they have been shown unto us by the power of God, and not of man. And we declare with words of soberness, that an angel of God came down from heaven, and he brought and laid before our eyes, that we beheld and saw the plates, and the engravings thereon; and we know that it is by the grace of God the Father, and our Lord Jesus Christ, that we beheld and bear record that these things are true. And it is marvelous in our eyes. Nevertheless, the voice of the Lord commanded us that we should bear record of it; wherefore, to be obedient unto the commandments of God, we bear testimony of these things. And we know that if we are faithful in Christ, we shall rid our garments of the blood of all men, and be found spotless before the judgment-seat of Christ, and shall dwell with him eternally in the heavens. And the honor be to the Father, and to the Son, and to the Holy Ghost, which is one God. Amen."

THE TESTIMONY OF EIGHT WITNESSES

"BE IT KNOWN unto all nations, kindreds, tongues, and people, unto whom this work shall come: That Joseph Smith, Jun., the translator of this work, has shown unto us the plates of which hath been spoken, which have the appearance of gold; and as many of the leaves as the said Smith has translated we did handle with our hands; and we also saw the engravings thereon, all of which has the appearance of ancient work, and of curious workmanship. And this we bear record with words of soberness, that the said Smith has shown unto us, for we have seen and hefted, and know of a surety that the said Smith has got the plates of which we have spoken. And we give our names unto the world, to witness unto the world that which we have seen. And we lie not, God bearing witness of it."

To their dying days, each of these witnesses held firm to what they had testified to be true concerning the Book of Mormon. One major factor that adds to the validity of their witnesses is that many of them, including all three of the Three Witnesses, became disaffected from Joseph Smith and the Church. Two of the three, Oliver Cowdery and Martin Harris, eventually returned to the Church and died as faithful members. Yet, even David Whitmer, who could never overcome his personal differences with Joseph Smith, never denied the testimony that he gave inside the cover of the Book of Mormon.

Two years prior to his death in 1875 and then again on his deathbed, Martin Harris gave this testimony: "I do say that the angel did show to me the plates containing the Book of Mormon. . . . I do firmly believe and do know that Joseph Smith was a prophet of God" (*Saint's Herald,* 22:630).

A year and a half before his death, after rejoining the church, Oliver Cowdery addressed a large audience concerning the Book of Mormon. He said, "I beheld with my eyes, and handled with my hands, the gold plates from which it was translated. I also beheld the interpreters. That book is true" (Anderson, *Investigating the Book of Mormon Witnesses,* 61). A dozen of Oliver's relatives left memories of his last moments, when he reassured his wife, daughter, and close family members of his love for Christ, of the truthfulness of the Book of Mormon, and of the reality of the restoration of the priesthood (see *Book of Mormon Reference Companion,* 790).

David Whitmer lived until 1888. He was a respected businessman in Richmond, Missouri. There he was interviewed often by journalists seeking information concerning his testimony published in the Book of Mormon. He published numerous statements reiterating his testimony of the Book of Mormon and explained why he believed Joseph Smith had lost his gift of inspiration. In his last year of life he corrected encyclopedia accounts alleging that the three witnesses renounced their written testimony. He stated, "I will say once more to all mankind, that I have never, at any time denied that testimony or any part thereof" (Whitmer, *An Address to All believers in Christ*, 8). In his last hours of life, he followed the pattern set by Oliver and Martin; he bore witness that the Book of Mormon was given by God.

Before reviewing the testimonies of the Eight Witnesses, it would be well to look at a single verse in the book of Matthew in the New Testament. Jesus spoke a one-verse parable that has significance to Latter-day Saints concerning the Three Witnesses. Matthew wrote, "Another parable spake he unto them; The kingdom of heaven is like unto leaven, which a woman took, and hid in three measures of meal, till the whole was leavened" (Matthew 13:33). Are the three hidden measures of meal that leaven the kingdom of heaven the Three Witnesses of the Book of Mormon?

Elder Bruce R. McConkie, commenting on this parable, referred to a statement made by the Prophet Joseph Smith: "Although the Parable of the Leaven applies in principle to the growth of faith and testimony in the hearts of men in any age, it also has an express application to the setting up of the latter-day kingdom. 'It may be understood,' the Prophet Joseph Smith explained, 'that the Church of the Latter-day Saints has taken its rise from a little leaven that was put into three witnesses. Behold, how much this is like the parable! It is fast leavening the lump, and will soon leaven the whole'" (*Doctrinal New Testament Commentary*, 299; Smith, *Teachings*, 1977, 100).

Joseph Smith Sr., Hyrum Smith, and Samuel Smith all died faithful in the Church and never denied their witness of the Book of Mormon. In fact, Hyrum and Samuel both laid down their lives for their testimonies. Members of the Whitmer family, including Hiram Page, went to their graves proclaiming the truthfulness of the plates and the divine nature of the Book of Mormon—even though four were excommunicated from the Church (see *Book of Mormon Reference Companion*, 791).

Why would anyone who has studied the lives and testimonies of these eleven men not take seriously the existence of the gold plates and the validity of the Book of Mormon? Perhaps, at least in part, the reason can be explained by a scripture story from the New Testament and one verse from the book of Mormon.

"There was a certain rich man, which was clothed in purple and fine linen, and fared sumptuously every day: And there was a certain beggar named Lazarus, which was laid at his gate, full of sores, And desiring to be fed with the crumbs which fell from the rich man's table: moreover the dogs came and licked his sores.

"And it came to pass, that the beggar died, and was carried by the angels into Abraham's bosom: the rich man also died, and was buried; and in hell he lift up his eyes, being in torments, and seeth Abraham afar off, and Lazarus in his bosom.

"And he cried and said, Father Abraham, have mercy on me, and send Lazarus, that he may dip the tip of his finger in water, and cool my tongue; for I am tormented in this flame.

"But Abraham said, Son, remember that thou in thy lifetime receivedst thy good things, and likewise Lazarus evil things: but now he is comforted, and thou art tormented.

"And beside all this, between us and you there is a great gulf fixed: so that they which would pass from hence to you cannot; neither can they pass to us, that would come from thence.

"Then he said, I pray thee therefore, father, that thou wouldest send him to my father's house: For I have five brethren;

that he may testify unto them, lest they also come into this place of torment.

"Abraham saith unto him, They have Moses and the prophets; let them hear them. And he said, Nay, father Abraham: but if one went unto them from the dead, they will repent.

"And he said unto him, If they hear not Moses and the prophets, neither will they be persuaded, though one rose from the dead" (Luke 16:19–31).

Verse thirty-one reveals much about human tendency. If people won't believe Moses and the other prophets (or eleven witnesses), why would they believe Joseph Smith even if he showed them the gold plates or put them on display in a museum? They probably wouldn't. Jesus taught in this parable that even if someone came from the dead, it would be difficult for many to believe. (In the next charge against the Book of Mormon, I will discuss what some of the biblical prophets have said concerning the Book of Mormon and its coming forth in the latter days.)

In the Book of Mormon we learn a principle similar to that taught in Luke 16 about Lazarus and the rich man. "For in that day, for my sake shall the Father work a work, which shall be a great and a marvelous work among them; and there shall be among them those who will not believe it, although a man shall declare it unto them" (3 Nephi 21:9). The evidence is solid that the gold plates were real and that Joseph Smith translated the Book of Mormon, but there continue to be many who will not believe it although many declare it unto them.

5. No Man Should Add to the Bible

The Charge: The Book of Mormon violates the decree given by John the Revelator that no man can add unto or take away from the Bible (see Revelation 22:18–19).

The Answer: By the Bible we mean the collection of writings that contain the records of divine revelation. The word itself is of Greek origin, being derived from *ta biblia*, "the books." In course of time *biblia*, a neuter plural, was regarded as a feminine singular, and in that way "the books" came to be spoken of as "the book." By the word *Bible*, therefore, we must understand not a single book but rather a divine library (see LDS Bible Dictionary, 622). Other words that come from the same roots are *library* and *bibliography*, both referring to a compilation of books, not a single volume.

The book referred to in Revelation 22:18–19 is not the Bible but the book of Revelation itself. The Bible did not become known as such until in 325 A.D. at the council of Nicaea, when a work began to canonize the "scriptures." It is believed to have been completed in 360 A.D. at the council of Laodocia. The Greek Septuagint was accepted for the Old Testament, and the criteria for the New Testament was that the books be written by one of the Apostles of Jesus or be written during the time of the Apostles.

Some believe that the book of Revelation was compiled in approximately 95–96 A.D. by the Apostle John on the Isle of Patmos. Other scholars believe the time of writing to be closer to 60–70 A.D. Whichever group is right, scholars still place the writing of Revelation long before the councils canonized the book as scripture and added it to the Holy Bible. There is a common belief that John was writing futuristically and therefore meant the entire Bible. However, such thinking does not square with various religions that value the Bible as scripture. If it were true, then much of the Bible would be invalid as scripture because Moses, writing about his teachings and not the Bible as a whole, declared, "Ye shall not add unto the word which I command you, neither shall ye diminish ought from it, that ye may keep the commandments of the Lord your God which I command you" (Deuteronomy 4:2).

With this understanding, we can see that the Book of Mormon actually supports the idea of not adding to or taking away from the book of Revelation. In 1 Nephi 14, a prophet named Nephi is shown a vision of the future of the world but is forbidden to write all that he saw because he is instructed that that would be the job of one John, who would write the "revelation" in the future. The Book of Mormon states:

"And it came to pass that the angel spake unto me, saying: Look!

"And I looked and beheld a man, and he was dressed in a white robe.

"And the angel said unto me: Behold one of the twelve apostles of the Lamb.

"Behold, he shall see and write the remainder of these things; yea, and

also many things which have been.

"And he shall also write concerning the end of the world.

"Wherefore, the things which he shall write are just and true; and behold they are written in the book which thou beheld proceeding out of the mouth of the Jew; and at the time they proceeded out of the mouth of the Jew, or, at the time the book proceeded out of the mouth of the Jew, the things which were written were plain and pure, and most precious and easy to the understanding of all men.

"And behold, the things which this apostle of the Lamb shall write are many things which thou hast seen; and behold, the remainder shalt thou see.

"But the things which thou shalt see hereafter thou shalt not write; for the Lord God hath ordained the apostle of the Lamb of God that he should write them.

"And also others who have been, to them hath he shown all things, and they have written them; and they are sealed up to come forth in their purity, according to the truth which is in the Lamb, in the own due time of the Lord, unto the house of Israel.

"And I, Nephi, heard and bear record, that the name of the apostle of the Lamb was John, according to the word of the angel.

"And behold, I, Nephi, am forbidden that I should write the remainder of the things which I saw and heard; wherefore the things which I have written sufficeth me; and I have written but a small part of the things which I saw" (1 Nephi 14:18–28).

The Book of Mormon, then, instead of adding to or taking away from the Bible is a testament that the Bible is true. The Doctrine and Covenants, another book of LDS scripture, teaches that one of the major purposes for the Book of Mormon is to testify to the world that the Bible is true and is the word of God, "proving to the world that the holy scriptures are true, and that God does inspire men and call them to his holy work in this age and generation, as well as in generations of old; thereby showing that he is the same God yesterday, today, and forever. Amen" (D&C 20:11–12).

The Book of Mormon testifies of this same truth. It testifies that one of its purposes, along with other Latter-day scriptures (the Doctrine and Covenants, Pearl of Great Price, and Joseph Smith translation of the Bible), and teachings of modern Apostles and prophets, is to testify that the Bible is true and should be followed in life as a pattern for living. It declares:

"And it came to pass that I beheld the remnant of the seed of my brethren, and also the book of the Lamb of God, which had proceeded forth from the mouth of the Jew, that it came forth from the Gentiles unto the remnant of the seed of my brethren.

"And after it had come forth unto them I beheld other books, which came forth by the power of the Lamb, from the

Gentiles unto them, unto the convincing of the Gentiles and the remnant of the seed of my brethren, and also the Jews who were scattered upon all the face of the earth, that the records of the prophets and of the twelve apostles of the Lamb are true" (1 Nephi 13:38–39).

The Book of Mormon is full of references to the validity of the Bible and in no way takes from or adds to it. It testifies of it. For more teachings from the Book of Mormon concerning the Bible, see 1 Nephi 13:20–29, 40–41; 2 Nephi 29:3–14; 3 Nephi 23:1; and Mormon 7:8–9.

The Bible also contains passages of scripture that refer to the Book of Mormon. Some readers may not agree that these verses are speaking of the Book of Mormon, but if they are not referring to the Book of Mormon, then are they referring to other unknown scriptures. Either way, there must be some explanation for them. The Church of Jesus Christ of Latter-day Saints declares that they refer to the Book of Mormon.

The great Old Testament prophet Isaiah foresaw the coming forth of the Book of Mormon. He wrote of the destruction of the Nephite nation and how the Nephite record would come forth out of the ground, or "dust." He said, "And thou shalt be brought down, and shalt speak out of the ground, and thy speech shall be low out of the dust, and thy voice shall be, as of one that hath a familiar spirit, out of the ground, and thy speech shall whisper out of the dust" (Isaiah 29:4). This is precisely what occurred.

The Nephites were annihilated, but their record was preserved and brought forth "out of the ground" by Joseph Smith. Furthermore, Isaiah prophesied of an incident involving Joseph Smith and Martin Harris during the translation of the Book of Mormon. Martin took some of the translated characters to a noted Egyptologist, Professor Charles Anthon. Professor Anthon, upon examining the characters, "stated that the translation was correct, more so than any he had before seen translated from the Egyptian." Martin then showed him other characters that were not yet translated, and he said they were "true characters." However, when Professor Anthon learned that the records had been delivered to Joseph Smith by "an angel of God," he tore up the signed certificate of authenticity and replied, "I cannot read a sealed book." He then asked Martin to bring the plates to him and he would translate them. Martin declined and took the characters to a Dr. Mitchell, who certified what Professor Anthon had said both "respecting the characters and the translation" (Joseph Smith–History 1:62–65).

Isaiah wrote of this incident. I have inserted names and the Book of Mormon for clarity. Isaiah said:

"And the vision of all is become unto you as the words of a book [the Book of Mormon] that is sealed, which *men* [Martin Harris] deliver to one that is learned [Professor Anthon], saying, Read this, I pray thee: and he saith, I cannot; for it is sealed. [Two-thirds of the gold plates were sealed, and Joseph was forbidden to translate them.]

"And the book [the Book of Mormon] is delivered to him that is not learned [Joseph Smith], saying, Read this, I pray thee: and he saith, I am not learned.

"Wherefore the Lord said, Forasmuch as this people draw near me with their mouth, and with their lips do honour me, but have removed their heart far from me, and their fear toward me is taught by the precept of men:

"Therefore, behold, I will proceed to do a marvellous work among this people, even a marvellous work and a wonder: [bringing forth of the Book of Mormon and The Church of Jesus Christ of Latter-day Saints] for the wisdom of their wise men shall perish, and the understanding of their prudent men shall be hid.

"Woe unto them that seek deep to hide their counsel from

the Lord, and their works are in the dark, and they say, Who seeth us? and who knoweth us?

"Surely your turning of things upside down shall be esteemed as the potter's clay: for shall the work say of him that made it, He made me not? or shall the thing framed say of him that framed it, He had no understanding?

"Is it not yet a very little while, and Lebanon shall be turned into a fruitful field, and the fruitful field shall be esteemed as a forest?

"And in that day shall the deaf hear the words of the book [the Book of Mormon], and the eyes of the blind shall see out of obscurity, and out of darkness" (Isaiah 29:11–18).

Isaiah is not the only Old Testament prophet who prophesied concerning the coming forth of the Book of Mormon. Ezekiel foresaw that God would prepare two records to gather scattered Israel home from their long dispersion. One was the stick of Judah (the Bible), and the other was the stick of Joseph (the Book of Mormon). He said that the two records would be joined together, "and they shall become one in thine hand." Concerning the use of the word *stick* in the Old Testament, there has been some speculation as to whether the sticks mentioned by Ezekiel were scrolls or tally sticks or actual wax writing boards (see Meservy, "Ezekiel's Sticks and the Gathering of Israel," 4–13; Nibley, *An Approach to the Book of Mormon,* 279–81). Regardless of what they were in Ezekiel's time, today they represent the Bible and the Book of Mormon working together in "one hand" to bring the fulness of the gospel of Christ to the people of the earth. Ezekiel wrote:

"The word of the Lord came again unto me, saying, Moreover, thou son of man, take thee one stick, and write upon it, For Judah, and for the children of Israel his companions: then take another stick, and write upon it, For Joseph, the stick of Ephraim, and *for* all the house of Israel his companions:

"And join them one to another into one stick; and they shall become one in thine hand.

"And when the children of thy people shall speak unto thee, saying, Wilt thou not shew us what thou *meanest* by these?

"Say unto them, Thus saith the Lord God; Behold, I will take the stick of Joseph, which is in the hand of Ephraim, and the tribes of Israel his fellows, and will put them with him, even with the stick of Judah, and make them one stick, and they shall be one in mine hand" (Ezekiel 37:15–19).

The gospel of John records Jesus as saying that he had other sheep that were not of the fold in and around Jerusalem (see John 10:15–16). Was Jesus testifying of the Book of Mormon people and others of the lost tribes of the House of Israel? The Book of Mormon records that that is precisely to whom Jesus was referring (see 3 Nephi 15:16–24). The Book of Mormon reveals that all people, those in the old world as well as in the new world, are valuable to Him, and He desires all to be one. He desires all to be "of one fold" and have "one shepherd." In 3 Nephi 15:21, Jesus declares to the inhabitants of the land Bountiful, after his resurrection in Palestine, "And verily I say unto you, that ye are they of whom I said: Other sheep I have which are not of this fold; them also I must bring, and they shall hear my voice; and there shall be one fold, and one shepherd."

The final scripture from the Bible that I will discuss referring to the Book of Mormon is Revelation 14:6–7. It reads: "And I saw another angel fly in the midst of heaven, having the everlasting gospel to preach unto them that dwell on the earth, and to every nation, and kindred, and tongue, and people,

"Saying with a loud voice, Fear God, and give glory to him; for the hour of his judgment is come: and worship him that made heaven, and earth, and the sea, and the fountains of waters."

Members of the Church of Jesus Christ of Latter-day Saints "identify this angel as Moroni, caretaker of Joseph's records and holder of 'the keys of the record of the stick of Ephraim' (D&C 27:5). Moroni heralded the Restoration and prepared Joseph Smith for his role in bringing forth God's great latter-day work" (*Book of Mormon Reference Companion*, 95).

The Book of Mormon, then, is not at odds with the Bible at all. It is a companion scripture that testifies that the Bible is true and that Jesus is the Christ. It does not add unto the book of Revelation, nor does it take away from it. The charge that the Book of Mormon violates John's decree in Revelation 22:18–19 simply is not founded and is not true.

6. Changes Made to the Text

The Charge: How can the Book of Mormon be the most correct or most perfect book on earth if there have been so many changes made to its text?

The Answer: Joseph Smith did say that the Book of Mormon was the most correct book on earth. He said, "I told the brethren that the Book of Mormon was the most correct of any book on earth, and the keystone of our religion, and a man would get nearer to God by abiding by its precepts, than by any other book" (Smith, *History of the Church*, 4:461; introduction to the Book of Mormon). I have already discussed the fact that if the Book of Mormon is a fraud, then the Church and Joseph Smith are frauds also. The Church stands or falls on the truthfulness of the Book of Mormon. Thus, it is the keystone of our religion. But there is a key principle that will shed light on the answer in the words "by abiding by its precepts." The message Joseph Smith is making is that it is the living of what is taught that makes the book correct. Author George Horton makes this principle clear when he states:

"Understanding the nature of the thousands of small

changes in the Book of Mormon may be helpful and interesting. In reality, though, the kind of stylistic accuracy achieved by these changes has little to do with what Joseph meant when he called the Book of Mormon the 'most correct of any book on earth' (*History of the Church*, 4:461.) His concept of correctness had nothing to do with accepted standards of grammar, spelling, or punctuation.

"Looking at one definition of the word *correct* as accepted during Joseph Smith's day may be enlightening. Webster's 1828 American Dictionary of the English Language defines *correct* as being "literally, set right, or made straight. Hence, right: conformable to truth, rectitude or propriety, or conformable to a just standard. . . . *Correct* manners correspond with the rules of morality and received notions of decorum . . . *correct* principles coincide with the truth" ("Understanding Textual Changes in the Book of Mormon," 28).

According to this concept, the Book of Mormon certainly meets the test of correctness, for its principles coincide with truth. And, as Joseph Smith himself explained, the ultimate test of its correctness is in the lives of those who use its principles in their lives. Indeed, he promised that we can "get nearer to God by abiding by its precepts, than by any other book" (Smith, *History of the Church*, 4:461).

Of course there have been thousands of changes made in the Book of Mormon. In punctuation and grammar alone there have been thirty to thirty-five thousand changes. We must remember that although Joseph Smith was the translator of the Book of Mormon, the spelling in the first edition was Oliver Cowdery's, and the punctuation was John H. Gilbert's, who was the typesetter. Gilbert worked for E. B. Grandin and was a non-Mormon. He took great liberty with the text and with interpreting Oliver Cowdery's handwriting. As a result, many changes needed to be made to get the text back to how it read in the original document. Also, the spelling and grammar of the time period in America had no particular rules and was not yet standardized in 1829. Because there have been so many changes to the text from the 1830 edition to the current 1981 edition, I have included some substantial quotes below from Horton's article, "Understanding Textual Changes in the Book of Mormon." The article covers the history of various editions of the Book of Mormon, American English spelling and grammar in 1829, major changes in the various editions, and the concept of correctness as touched on above.

Horton wrote concerning the major changes in the various editions of the Book of Mormon that, "We also need to remember that Oliver Cowdery wrote what he heard. Many of the words—Nephite and Lamanite names, for example—would have been unfamiliar to Oliver. Joseph apparently had to correct some of these proper nouns. Consider, too, that the two distinct words *strait* and *straight* would sound exactly the same as Joseph dictated it. But Oliver spelled both words *straight* every time. In ten places, *straight* had to be corrected to read *strait*.

"Oliver's handwriting also presented a special challenge to the typesetter. His *R* (which looks like a 'Palmer' *R*) and his *N* are difficult to distinguish, as are his *B* and *L*. So in the first edition, Gadianton was mislabeled "the *nobler*," rather than "the *robber*." In a similar way, the typesetter apparently mistook Oliver's *RM* as *UN*. So in 1 Nephi 13 [1 Ne. 13], where the original manuscript read *formation,* the typesetter misread *founation.* Then, thinking the letter *d* had been left out, he supplied it. In the 1981 edition, *foundation* has been corrected back to read *formation,* as originally intended.

"Many other spelling errors appear to have been strictly typographical, for example, *aaswer, amog, bacause, daghter, mnltitude, theit,* and *uttered.*

"Another kind of common copying error occurred when the typesetter's eye momentarily left the page. Then, when he looked back, he would pick up the text at a different spot where the wording was very similar. The most significant example of this is the dropping of thirty-five words in Alma 32:30, where the words *seed, good, sprouteth, beginneth,* and *grow* are common to two parts of the verse.

"Some of the words we thought Oliver Cowdery misspelled are actually legitimate variants found in the venerable *Oxford English Dictionary.* Consider these: *adhear, adultry, babtized, befal, burthensome, centre, condescention, devlish, fraid, phrensied,* and *sepulcher.*

"But the most common changes have not been in spelling, but in grammar. For example, there have been 891 changes of *which* to *who,* 177 changes of *exceeding* to *exceedingly.* Many changes involve a change in number or tense of verbs. *Was* was changed to *were* 162 times, *is* to *are* 74 times, and *done* to *did* 10 times.

"A few other changes involving meaning appear to be more significant. In 2 Nephi 30:6, *white* appeared in the 1830 and 1837 editions. Joseph changed this word to *pure* in the 1840 edition. But later American editions did not show this change because they had followed the first European and 1837 editions. This correction by the Prophet has finally been restored in the 1981 edition.

"In Mosiah 21:28 and Ether 4:1, the first edition had "Benjamin" where the name of Mosiah now appears. In fact, King Benjamin would not likely have still been living in the historical period described by these verses. In the 1837 edition, the Prophet Joseph made this correction.

"We can only speculate about the cause of this error. Book of Mormon scholar Sidney B. Sperry has posed this interesting question: "Was it an inadvertent slip of the tongue on the part of Joseph Smith as he dictated his translation to Oliver Cowdery, or did he translate correctly an original error on the part of Mormon, the abridger of the Book of Mormon? (*The Problems of the Book of Mormon*, Salt Lake City: Bookcraft, 1964, p. 203.)

"Over the years, a few hundred deletions have also been made, primarily to improve the book grammatically. The most commonly eliminated have been the words *that* (188 times), *the* (48 times), *it came to pass* (46 times), *a* and *and* (40 times), and *had* (29 times).

"Additions have been less numerous, probably less than one hundred. For example, *of* was added 12 times, *and, is,* and *the* 7 times. Some additions simply result from rearranging parts of a sentence or returning words inadvertently dropped in earlier editions. These are not "true" additions.

"In a few places, however, Joseph Smith did intentionally add to the text to clarify a point. An illustration of this is the added words *the son of* in 1 Nephi 11:21, 32 and 13:40. The text would be correct with or without the additional words, but the addition helps the reader avoid misunderstanding" (for further explanation of the numerous changes made through the various editions of the Book of Mormon, see, Horton, "Understanding Textual Changes in the Book of Mormon,"Ensign, December 1983, 24-28).

We should remember that Moroni, on the title page of the Book of Mormon, wrote to all readers of the book, "And now, if there are faults they are the mistakes of men; wherefore, condemn not the things of God, that ye may be found spotless at the judgment-seat of Christ." We learn from Ether 12:23–27 that this same Moroni was worried, as he wrote his portion of the record, that "the Gentiles will mock at these things because of our weakness in writing; for Lord thou has made us mighty in word by faith, but thou hast not made us mighty in writing."

He continued, "When we write we behold our weakness, and stumble because of the placing of our words; and I fear that the Gentiles will mock at our words." The Lord responds to Moroni by assuring him, "Fools mock, but they shall mourn; and my grace is sufficient for the meek, that they shall take no advantage of your weakness." It is imperative that we be meek and humble as we study the Book of Mormon. Then the grace of the Lord will be sufficient for each of us.

7. No DNA Evidence

The Charge: The introduction to the Book of Mormon states that the Book of Mormon people who were not destroyed by war are the "principal ancestors of the American Indians." Yet there is no DNA evidence that connects Hebrew DNA with that of the American Indians.

The Answer: The web page for FARMS, the Foundation for Ancient Research and Mormon Studies, states, "In recent times, some critics have suggested that there is a simple way to determine the validity of the Book of Mormon by the analysis and comparison of Hebrew and American Indian DNA. Some have even suggested that such studies have already been done and that they showed no genetic relationship between the two peoples. In reality, much research still needs to be done, but it seems unlikely that such research could provide evidence for or against the Book of Mormon. We do not know what ancient Israelite or Nephite/Lamanite DNA looked like, and modern Jewish populations may not reflect Israelite ancestry because of intermarriage and conversion over the past few thousand years" (see http://farms.byu.edu/publications/dna.php?selectio n=dna&cat=dna).

In addition, the American Indians may not have been the only people who lived in the Americas during Book of Mormon times. When considering the phrase "the principal ancestors of the Americana Indians," it would be good to review the meaning of *principal*. Webster's dictionary defines principal as the highest rank, character, or importance. The Book of Mormon does not claim to be a record of all the inhabitants of the Americas. In fact, some scholars believe that there were people from many lands in the Americas (see Sorenson, *An Ancient American Setting for the Book of Mormon;* Nibley, *The Prophetic Book of Mormon*).

Because DNA research is still ongoing, I refer you to several articles on the subject (see the Web address listed above). The articles included on this site address different issues related to the DNA question as it relates to Book of Mormon peoples.

8. Use of the Word Adieu

The Charge: The Book of Mormon is a fraud because Jacob 7:27 ends with the word *adieu*, which is clearly of French origin. The French language was not developed for hundreds of years after the time of Jacob.

The Answer: Because the Book of Mormon is translation literature, the word *adieu* was Joseph Smith's word and not Jacob's. Daniel Ludlow gives a simple explanation that gives clear meaning to the use of a French word in the Book of Mormon. He comments:

"Such critics evidently overlook the fact that the Book of Mormon is translation literature, and Joseph Smith felt free in his translation to use any words familiar to himself and his readers that would best convey the meaning of the original author. It is interesting to note that there is a Hebrew word *Lehitra'ot,* which has essentially the same meaning in Hebrew as the word *adieu* has in French. Both of these words are much more than a simple farewell; they include the idea of a blessing. Would it be unreasonable to remind these critics that *none of the words* contained in the English translation of the book of

Jacob were used by Jacob himself? These words all come from the English language, which did not come into existence until long after Jacob's time (*A Companion to Your Study of the Book of Mormon*, 163)!

Conclusion

As this book comes to a close, it is not possible to cover every objection to the Book of Mormon or question that has been raised since its publication in 1830. However, I hope that the few that have been addressed have been helpful to the reader. As of February 2000 more than one hundred million copies of the book have been published in over 100 languages including American Sign Language. This will allow some 87 percent of the earth's several billion inhabitants to read the book in their own language (see *Book of Mormon Reference Companion*, 160). With that many people reading the book, numerous and various questions will be raised; such as the language in which the book was originally written, different writing styles incorporated in the book, and numerous questions about Mormons. One of the most common questions is "why are members of your church called Mormons? The name was given to the Church by people not of the faith. It was not originally intended as a compliment but had reference to the churches belief in the Book of Mormon. However, Joseph Smith declared that the word Mormon should be translated "more good." President Gordon B. Hinckley commented on this definition. He said, "Mormon Should Mean "More Good." He then quoted Joseph as saying, "Look, if there is any name that is totally honorable in its derivation, it is the name Mormon. And so, when someone asks me about it and what it means, I quietly say—'Mormon means more good.' " (The Prophet Joseph Smith first said this in 1843; see Times and Seasons, 4:194; Teachings of the Prophet Joseph Smith, pp. 299-300.) President Hinckley then said," His statement intrigued me—Mormon means "more good." I knew, of course, that "more good" was not a derivative of the word Mormon. I had studied both Latin and Greek, and I knew that English is derived in some measure from those two languages and that the words more good are not a cognate of the word Mormon. But his was a positive attitude based on an interesting perception. And, as we all know, our lives are guided in large measure by our perceptions. Ever since, when I have seen the word Mormon used in the media to describe us—in a newspaper or a magazine or book or whatever—there flashes into my mind his statement, which has become my motto: Mormon means "more good" (President Gordon B. Hinckley, "More Good", Ensign, November 1990, 51). Therefore, when members of The Church of Jesus Christ of Latter-day Saints are referred to as "Mormons," it is not offensive. Hopefully all of us will desire to live a life that exemplifies "more good."

As mentioned earlier in the text, the real question that must be answered and solved for every individual is, was Joseph Smith a true prophet of God? If he was, and I testify that he was, then the Book of Mormon is true. It is difficult to understand why the Christian world does not, for the most part, accept the Book of Mormon as scripture when the claims against it are unfounded, and the sweet spirit that comes from it brings much peace and direction to life. President Hinckley has asked the same question: "I knew a so-called intellectual who said the Church was trapped by its history. My response was that without that history we have nothing. The truth of that unique, singular, and remarkable event is the pivotal substance of our faith.

"But this glorious [First] vision was but the beginning of a series of manifestations that constitute the early history of this work.

"As if that vision were not enough to certify to the personality and the reality of the Redeemer of mankind, there followed the coming forth of the Book of Mormon. Here is something that a man could hold in his hands, could 'heft,' as it were. He could read it. He could pray about it, for it contained a promise that the Holy Ghost would declare its truth if that witness were sought in prayer.

"This remarkable book stands as a testimonial to the living reality of the Son of God. The Bible declares that 'in the mouth of two or three witnesses every word may be established' (Matthew 18:16). The Bible, the testament of the Old World, is one witness. The Book of Mormon, the testament of the New World, is another witness.

"I cannot understand why the Christian world does not accept this book. I would think they would be looking for anything and everything that would establish without question the reality and the divinity of the Savior of the world" ("The Marvelous Foundation of Faith," 80–81).

I testify that that is exactly what the Book of Mormon will do for anyone who will be an honest seeker of truth. It will bring more light and knowledge as to the divinity of the Savior of the world. My closing message is the same as that found in the final two paragraphs of the introduction page to the Book of Mormon. It reads:

"We invite all men everywhere to read the Book of Mormon, to ponder in their hearts the message it contains, and then to ask God, the Eternal Father, in the name of Christ if the book is true. Those who pursue this course and ask in faith will gain a testimony of its truth and divinity by the power of the Holy Ghost" (Moroni 10:3–5).

Those who gain this divine witness from the Holy Spirit will also come to know by the same power that Jesus Christ is the Savior of the world, that Joseph Smith is His revelator and prophet in these last days, and that The Church of Jesus Christ of Latter-day Saints is the Lord's kingdom once again established on the earth, preparatory to the second coming of the Messiah.

Bibliography

Allen, Joseph L. *Book of Mormon Reference Companion* Salt Lake City: Deseret Book, 2003, 668–70.

Anderson, Richard L. *Investigating the Book of Mormon Witnesses.* Salt Lake City: Deseret Book, 1981.

Benson, Ezra Taft. *A Witness and a Warning.* Salt Lake City: Deseret Book, 1988.

Black, Susan Easton. *Finding Christ through the Book of Mormon.* Salt Lake City:

Deseret Book, 1987.

Hinckley, Gordon B. "'An Angel from on High, the Long, Long Silence Broke," *Ensign*, November 1979, 7–9.

_____. "An Unending Conflict, a Victory Assured," *Ensign,* June 2007, 4–9.

_____. "A Testimony Vibrant and True," *Ensign*, August 2005, 2–6.

_____. "The Cornerstones of Our Faith," *Ensign,* November 1984, 50–53.

_____. "The Marvelous Foundation of Faith, *Ensign*, November 2002, 80–81.

_____. "Power of the Book of Mormon," *Ensign,* June 1988, 2–6.

Horton, George. "Understanding Textual Changes in the Book of Mormon," *Ensign,* December 1983, 24–28.

Jessee, Dean. "Among Historians," *Ensign*, September 1979, 57–61.

Largey, Dennis L. *Book of Mormon Reference Companion*. Salt Lake City: Deseret Book, 2003.

Ludlow, Daniel. *A Companion to Your Study of the Book of Mormon*. Salt Lake City: Deseret Book, 1976.

McConkie, Bruce R. *Doctrinal New Testament Commentary*, 3 volumes, Salt Lake City: Bookcraft, 1973.

_____. *Millennial Messiah*. Salt Lake City: Deseret Book, 1982.

_____. "What Think Ye of the Book of Mormon?" *Ensign*, November 1983, 72–74.

McConkie, Joseph Fielding, and Craig J. Ostler. *Revelations of the Restoration: A Commentary on the Doctrine and Covenants and Other Modern Revelations*. Salt Lake City: Deseret Book, 2000.

Meservy, Keith H. "Ezekiel's Sticks and the Gathering of Israel." *Ensign*, February 1987, 4–13.

Newell, Linda King, Avery, Valeen Tippets, *Mormon Enigma: Emma Hale Smith*, Champaign, Illinois, University of Illinois Press, 1994.

Nibley, Hugh. *An Approach to the Book of Mormon*. Salt Lake City: Deseret News Press, 1957.

_____. *The Prophetic Book of Mormon*. Provo, Utah: FARMS, 2004.

Pratt, Parley P. *Autobiography of Parley P. Pratt*. Edited by Scot Facer Proctor and Maurine Jensen Proctor. Salt Lake City: Deseret Book, 2000.

Roberts, B. H. *A Comprehensive History of The Church of Jesus Christ of Latter-day Saints*, 6 vols. Provo, Utah: Brigham Young University Press, 1976.

Saints' Herald 22, no. 20 (15 October 1875); 26, no. 19 (1 October 1879). **[page numbers?]**

Smith, Joseph. *History of The Church of Jesus Christ of Latter-day Saints*. Edited by B. H. Roberts. 7 vols., 2d ed. rev. Salt Lake City: Deseret Book, 1932–51.

_____. *Teachings of the Prophet Joseph Smith*. Compiled by Joseph Fielding Smith. Salt Lake City: Deseret Book, 1976.

Smith, Joseph Fielding. *Doctrines of Salvation*. 3 vols. Salt Lake City: Bookcraft, 1974.

Smith, Lucy Mack. *Biographical Sketches of Joseph Smith, the Prophet, and His Progenitors for Many Generations*. Liverpool: S. W. Richards, 1853.

Sorenson, John L. *An Ancient American Setting for the Book of Mormon*. Salt Lake City: Deseret Book, 1985.

_____. *Images of Ancient America: Visualizing Book of Mormon Life*. Provo, Utah: FARMS Research Press, 1998.

Washburn, J. Nile. *Book of Mormon Lands and Times*. Bountiful, Utah: Horizon Publishers, 1974.

Whitmer, David. *An Address to All Believers in Christ*. Richmond, Mo.: N.p., 1887.

Widstoe, John A. *Evidences and Reconciliation*. Salt Lake City: Bookcraft, 1943.

About the Author

Jack R. Christianson was raised in Orem, Utah, and currently resides there. He is married to Melanie Harris. They are the parents of four daughters and are the grandparents of five grandsons and five granddaughters.

He graduated from Weber State University with a teaching degree in English and physical education. He received a master's degree in educational administration from Brigham Young University and a Ph.D. in educational sociology from the University of Buckingham.

He has taught classes on the Book of Mormon for the Church Educational System of The Church of Jesus Christ of Latter-day Saints for many years. While doing so, he served as the director of the Orem Institute of Religion, located adjacent to Utah Valley State College, and as a visiting scholar at Brigham Young University. He currently is an Administrator at Utah Valley State College in Orem, Utah.

He has written several books for the LDS market and two for a general audience. He has also published numerous talks on tape and CD.

He has served in the LDS Church in numerous capacities, including missionary, bishop, and stake president.

SETTING THE RECORD STRAIGHT SERIES

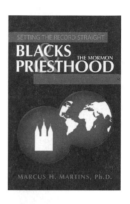

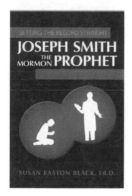

To learn more about these and other Millennial Press
titles, visit www.millennialpress.com. To purchase
these books visit your local bookstore.